A Meech Lake Post-Mortem

A Meech Lake Post-Mortem

Is Quebec Sovereignty Inevitable?

Pierre Fournier

Translated from the French
by Sheila Fischman

McGill-Queen's University Press
Montreal & Kingston • London • Buffalo

© McGill-Queen's University Press 1991
ISBN 0-7735-0866-x (cloth)
ISBN 0-8835-0867-8 (paper)

Legal deposit second quarter 1991
Bibliothèque nationale du Québec

Printed in Canada

This book is a translation of *Autopsie du Lac Meech: La
souveraineté, est-elle inévitable?* published by VLB Éditeur
1990. Translation and publication have been assisted by
grants from the Canada Council.

Canadian Cataloguing in Publication Data

Fournier, Pierre, 1947–
A Meech Lake post-mortem
Translation of: Autopsie du Lac Meech
ISBN 0-7735-0866-x (bound).–
ISBN 0-7735-0867-8 (pbk.).
1. Canada. Constitution Amendment, 1987.
2. Federal-provincial relations–Quebec (Province).
3. Quebec (Province)–History–Autonomy and independence
movements. 4. Federal government–Canada. I. Title.
JL65 1990.F6813 1991   342′.03   C91-090097-3
64747

This book was typeset in Caledonia 10.5/13
by Caractéra inc., Quebec City.

Contents

Acknowledgments

My special thanks to Josée Legault of the Université du Québec à Montréal, who was responsible for the research and a good part of the writing in chapters 2 and 3, and who contributed a great deal to the correction and revision of the text. Many thanks also to Sheila Fischman who translated the French version diligently and competently.

I'd be remiss if I didn't acknowledge the contributions of Jean Chrétien, Clyde Wells, Pierre Trudeau, and Elijah Harper. By speeding the course of history, they gave me the motivation and the courage I needed to spend my first post-Meech summer out of the sun.

P.F.

This translation had to be produced very quickly, and I couldn't have done it alone. Graham Fraser of *The Globe and Mail* helped me with unfamiliar terminology, and Stephen Godfrey of the same newspaper sent me many column-inches of Meech Lake coverage. I am grateful to both of them, and to the author of this book, Pierre Fournier, who was a model of patience, lent me books from his library, and provided me with some of the original English quotations.

S.F.

Introduction

Why a post-mortem of the still-warm corpse of Meech Lake? Because, looking beyond the legal jargon and the constitutional battles, the endless debates on the accord can be seen to have been both a formidable detonator and a powerful revelation of what Quebec and English Canada have become.

For the Québécois, Meech Lake has had the tremendous advantage of clarifying what is at stake in their collective destiny. Never have the chief political forces in Canada shown themselves in so harsh a light as they did over those three long years. Never have the different realities and irreconcilable visions underlying this country's existence been so obvious. Never has the gulf between Quebec's aspirations and English Canada's been so deep. And above all, never has the present Quebec government revealed so clearly its deepest intentions for the future of Quebec.

Pierre Trudeau's genius lay in camouflaging Canada's incompatibilities and contradictions for almost two decades, thereby making possible the momentary triumph of a vision that matched neither the reality nor the aspirations of either Quebec or English Canada. Even if the former prime minister emerged victorious from the Meech round – after having contributed in large measure to its failure – this farce at least helped demystify the man and his ideas. An ally of the most reactionary and most anti-francophone elements in Canadian society, Trudeau would finally be unmasked to the Québécois, who were now ready to purge themselves of the influence of the man who, more than anyone else, had stood in the way of the normal evolution of Quebec. My re-examination of the Trudeau legacy will deal in particular with the years 1980–82, following the referendum victory, when he managed to fool Quebec by reneging on his promise of "renewed federalism" and by saddling Quebec with a constitution it quite obviously didn't want.

In chapter 2 I shall attempt to show that the suggestion by the current Quebec government and most analysts that, overall, Meech Lake offered an acceptable compromise does not stand up to analysis. A close examination of the minimum demands of 1986, of the June 1987 accord, and of the June 1990 concessions reveals that Quebec's interests would in no way have been served by the ratification of a document that, at several levels, would have led to major setbacks for Quebec. With the help of a brief historical survey, I shall then examine the main plot turns in this bad soap opera – in which reality was often stranger than fiction – leaving it to others to take stock of all its consequences.

We shall see that the principal reasons for English Canada's rejection of the accord, including the rights of linguistic minorities, Bill 178, the role of native peoples and ethnic groups, and Senate reform, were merely pretexts aimed at concealing feelings and attitudes that were profoundly anti-francophone and anti-Quebec. The accord's opponents, although their ideas were rarely convincing, only managed to preach to the converted precisely because they were so adept at exploiting deeply held prejudices regarding Quebec.
At the same time, one of the great revelations of the debate was the appearance of an English Canada that, although in a muddled and contradictory manner, is desperately in search of itself, and seems to be forging a consensus about its own collective destiny. If there are still some who think that English Canada won't survive the sovereignty of Quebec, reading this book should persuade them otherwise. What is more, unlike

the 1980 referendum period when English Canada seemed prepared to make important compromises, it now insists that Quebec's inclusion be based on the constitutional status quo with no recognition, symbolic or real, of its specific nature.

Are nationalist stirrings in Quebec only a flash in the pan, or do they represent a genuine turning-point in its political evolution? The three final chapters will attempt to answer this question, while summing up the post-Meech political, economic, and linguistic situations. Beginning with an analysis of the challenges and constraints that Quebec must meet in this final decade of the twentieth century, I will suggest that although present circumstances are exceptional there are still considerable obstacles to sovereignty. Despite the efforts and progress made in recent years, the future of the French language is still far from certain. Economically, Quebec now has the means to become sovereign. This won't stop the debate over the next months and years from revolving once again around the economic viability of an independent Quebec. And as far as the political outcome is concerned, those who think that the march towards sovereignty is inevitable or ineluctable, and that the present government of Quebec will be in charge of the project, are in danger of a rude awakening.

A Meech Lake Post-Mortem

– I –

The Trudeau Legacy

Others are more qualified than I to go back to the Conquest to search for the underlying meaning of the Meech Lake epic. I shall simply present a shorter and necessarily more superficial historical review that will attempt to demonstrate the importance of the referendum and the 1982 patriation of the Canadian constitution to an explanation of the Meech saga and the present situation.

By the early 1980s, Quebec's future seemed rather bleak. For most Quebec nationalists, the failure of the referendum had led to bitterness, defeatism, and demobilization. The victory of the "No" side, which to most analysts at the time seemed to signal the final stage in the decline of nationalism, must be seen today as one more step towards a new political status for Quebec.

In fact, that "victory" turned out to be fairly superficial. A good number of francophones who had voted "No" still identified themselves as "Québécois first." They felt no socio-political ties to Canada, but were concerned about economic insecurity in an economy heavily controlled by Anglo-Canadians and Americans. Their fears, which affected mainly the most disadvantaged members of our society, had been skilfully exploited. A scare campaign centred largely on federal unemployment-insurance, family allowance, and old-age pension cheques had been devastatingly effective. But support won through fear is necessarily fragile, humiliating and temporary. When circumstances change and fears evaporate, people change course with unfeigned enthusiasm. Just ask the Eastern Europeans.

THE LIE OF "RENEWED FEDERALISM"

The cost of defeating the "Yes" side was the promise of an in-depth renewal of federalism. On the night of 16 May 1980, four days before the referendum, Pierre Trudeau spoke at Montreal's Paul Sauvé arena. He made a solemn commitment, in his own name and in the names of the Conservatives, the NDP, his Liberal caucus, and the nine other provinces, to renew federalism. He claimed that the federal Liberal MPs from Quebec were even prepared to "put their seats on the line to bring about change." Trudeau himself took part in the later controversy over the meaning of this promise. He did his utmost to show that "renewed federalism" never meant anything except repatriation, the Charter of Rights, and a new centralizing thrust. The stakes were important, because he was gambling both his credibility and his place in history.

Only through a close analysis of the referendum context can we uncover the true meaning of this promise for the Québécois at the time. Hundreds of declarations over the months and weeks leading up to the referendum leave no doubt as to the general understanding of renewed federalism: greater autonomy for Quebec to ensure its linguistic and cultural development, a concept that had been part of the list of demands of every Quebec premier since 1960. A CROP/Radio-Canada poll showed that the majority of Québécois preferred the option of "renewed federalism".[1] In addition, 56 percent of respondents were of the opinion that provincial powers should be increased, and 51 percent thought Quebec should have special powers, different from the other provinces, in certain fields, notably language (66 percent of respondents in favour), culture (64 percent), and natural resources (56 percent). The Québécois wanted and expected major constitutional changes.

4

Two years before the referendum, the Commission on Canadian Unity created by Trudeau had crossed the country from east to west. The Pépin-Robarts report, tabled in 1979, confirmed Quebec's right to self-determination and upheld the idea that the province should have broader powers, because it constituted "the stronghold of the French-Canadian people." It suggested as well that the residual power should be granted to the provinces, which could opt out of federal government programs and receive fiscal compensation. Furthermore, the provinces would be given responsibility for their minorities.

A few months before the referendum, on 9 January 1980, Claude Ryan, leader of the Quebec Liberal Party and of the "No" side, tabled a document which highlighted the main components of renewed federalism. While it did not advocate "special status," the Beige Paper nonetheless clearly promoted decentralization and a reinforcement of Quebec's powers. In particular, it contained proposals aimed at limiting Ottawa's unilateral powers, instituting a dualist federal council, giving the provinces control over broadcasting, and increasing Quebec's "cultural sovereignty."

The Beige Paper was well received not only by the majority of the non-sovereignist political forces in Quebec, but also by the Liberal Party of Canada. Jean Chrétien spoke of a "judicious and realistic document that made some very good proposals." Jeanne Sauvé even declared that by "recommending greater decentralization, most of the proposals contained in the document are compatible with the thinking of the federal Liberal leader, Pierre Trudeau."[2]

Then it was the turn of the premiers of the English-speaking provinces, notably Bill Davis, Brian Peckford and Richard Hatfield, to heap praise on the Beige Paper. For Peckford: "Quebec will finally realize that it is in its interest to stay in a renewed confederation in which the advantages and virtues of strong provincial social entities will be defended by all the provinces rather than by Quebec alone."[3]

Less specifically, while admitting that his province's position was part of "a strategy aimed at fighting plans for sovereignty-association during the referendum," Ontario Intergovernmental Affairs Minister Thomas Wells greeted the Ryan proposal as "a reasonable, positive and constructive contribution."[4]

As for Trudeau, he described the Beige Paper as "an extremely serious basis for discussion." And never throughout the referendum campaign did he repudiate the document or statements by numerous spokespersons for the "No" side about what renewed federalism would consist of. Indeed, three weeks before the referendum the prime minister, denying that he was in favour of the status quo, confirmed that the Beige Paper, the Pépin-Robarts report, and the provinces' proposals were all an interesting basis for the renewal of federalism.[5]

If the Québécois did not clearly grasp Trudeau's intentions at the time, there was good reason! The former prime minister was knowingly and brilliantly cultivating ambiguity and fostering confusion. He encouraged voters to accept a concept of renewed federalism that he was quick to repudiate *after* the referendum. Some, including René Lévesque and most clear-sighted political observers, weren't taken in by Trudeau's apparent change of direction. Others, however, including Ryan and a good number of the "No" supporters, were convinced that the promise was genuine and that the federal government was prepared to make some concessions towards Quebec's historical demands. It should have come as no surprise, then, that a number of Québécois felt betrayed in 1981 when Trudeau tabled his plan to patriate the constitution. The belief that the referendum promise had not been kept was now shared by the majority of Quebec federalists and by the Mulroney government.

In 1989 even *La Presse* editorial writer Marcel Adam accused Trudeau of having acted "fraudulently" towards Quebec when he passed the 1982 Constitution Act to fulfil his promise of renewed federalism. Stung to the quick, the former prime minister proceeded to launch a virulent but very enlightening polemic in which Claude Morin, notably, took part. Because Trudeau had always attempted to attribute to "separatists" alone any "errors in interpretation" of his idea of renewed federalism, it is both ironic and revealing that the object of his fury and contempt should have been Adam. For Adam, whom Trudeau described as a "nationalist in a pique," had for many years displayed a federalist orthodoxy unequalled in Quebec journalism. Indeed, in the days and weeks preceding the referendum, Adam had written a number of emotional pleas in favour of the "No" side and of Trudeau (see in particular his editorial of 16 May 1980). Adam had also demonstrated his profound conviction that federalism would be renewed in the sense in which most Québécois desired it. Yet that same Marcel Adam, whose political convictions have not changed since the referendum, now considers that he was misled by Trudeau at the time of patriation.

During this controversy Trudeau maintained correctly that it wouldn't have been logical for the defeat of the "Yes" to be followed by reforms of a kind that would please the "Yes" camp, even though a true statesman would have found a way to move towards "national reconciliation." What is abhorrent, however, is that he betrayed his own supporters, those who voted "No" to sovereignty but "Yes" to renewed federalism. In this debate, Trudeau managed to brush aside the essential questions. How did the majority of Québécois interpret the promise of "renewed federalism"? To what degree did he contribute directly or indirectly to maintaining the confusion about the meaning of renewed federalism? Did the 1982 patriation respond to the desire for a renewal of federalism expressed by the majority of Québécois?

PATRIATION: A TIME BOMB

The former prime minister contends that the Constitutional Act of 1982 was desired by the majority of Québécois. But what mandate did he have? A few months before the referendum he had regained power from Joe Clark, being careful to give no details on what the Constitutional Act might contain. At the time of the referendum, the renewed federalism proposed in the Act was altogether different from what the prime minister had promised. Moreover, surveys at the time showed that the Quebec population was strongly opposed to patriation. According to CROP, in March 1981 only 27 percent of respondents supported patriation, 54 percent were opposed, and 19 percent had no opinion. Later, in March 1982, opposition had remained remarkably stable: 26 percent in favour, 55 percent opposed, and 19 percent with no opinion.[6]

In an attempt to justify his position, Trudeau later quoted three other polls.[7] On 5 May 1982, *The Globe and Mail* published a Sorecom poll in which 75 percent of Québécois declared that it was important for Quebec to remain in Canada. Trudeau neglected to mention that this same poll showed that 61 percent of Québécois felt that the new Constitution had weakened Quebec's position in confederation, as opposed to 17 percent who thought the opposite.[8] On 19 June, *La Presse* published the findings of a Gallup poll which showed that 49 percent of Québécois believed that "in the long term, the 1982 Canadian constitution would be a good thing for Canada."[9] Ignoring the fact that the question is asked about Canada and not Quebec, Trudeau brushed aside the fine points, and deduced that the Québécois were in favour of unilateral patriation. Finally, he cited as proof another Gallup survey, published in *La Presse* on 15 December 1982, which showed that 58 percent of Québécois believed that "Confederation would not break up."[10] Of course this was only a prediction. In fact, every time the Québécois were asked to assess the validity of the way Trudeau had proceeded, they declared themselves opposed. The former prime minister prefaced his argument by stating that polls were not his strong point. There's no argument on that.

The discontent aroused by the constitutional *coup de force* led a number of Québécois nationalists who had voted "No" in the referendum to vote for the Parti Québécois in 1981. Until the introduction of the Constitution Act, the Quebec Liberals had had a wide lead in the polls. Shortly after that, they began to slip. Many Québécois, bitter and frustrated, chose to re-elect a government whose fundamental option had been defeated only a year before.

Under the circumstances, it's not surprising that, despite the importance of patriation, Trudeau had refused to appeal to the population on the matter. Considering the deep contempt he displays in his writing for the "democratic shortcomings" of the Québécois, one is entitled to be perplexed. The "separatists" at least had the decency to hold a referendum on their option.

When Trudeau, to justify his behavior, hid behind the Supreme Court, which had declared his unilateral patriation to be "legal" but not legitimate, it was the last straw. Considering his earlier denunciations in *Cité Libre* of the numerous injustices and aberrations at home and abroad that have been explained away in the name of legality, this argument is unworthy of him.

Trudeau's statements to the effect that the PQ government had tried at any price to abort constitutional negotiations in 1981 and 1982, and that it was responsible for the loss of Quebec's right of veto, don't stand up to analysis either. The Quebec government had certainly been clumsy and naive, but it still was able to reach an agreement with seven other provinces, and had even agreed to drop its veto *in exchange for* important concessions. Is that the behaviour of a government trying at all costs to abort a process? As for the right of veto, it had never been abandoned, in that the conditions attached to this concession were never accepted. One is entitled to wonder how Trudeau, as defender of Quebec's best interests, could agree without batting an eyelid to Quebec's loss of its veto. After all, wasn't he the one who was pulling the strings?

According to Gil Rémillard, the 1982 patriation insulted the Quebec government as a provincial government had never been insulted in the history of this country. In addition: "No Quebec government, regardless of its political allegiance, could have accepted this patriation. The argument that there was nothing to be done because the Quebec government was sovereignist doesn't stand up. René Lévesque led a legitimate government which on 2 October 1981 was given a clear mandate by the National Assembly to oppose any unilateral patriation by Ottawa."[11]

From the point of view of Canadian federalism and national unity, Meech Lake can be seen as a partial recognition of the errors committed by the Trudeau régime and as a modest attempt to "correct the injustice inflicted on Quebec"[12] by bringing Quebec back into Confederation, even if, as the former prime minister likes to emphasize, Quebec remained legally bound by the Constitution Act.

The grand victor, Trudeau, on the day after the referendum, took advantage of a highly exceptional set of circumstances: the independentists had been brought to heel and there was unprecedented good will in English Canada. Rather than working towards "national reconciliation," either in Canada or in Quebec, he reacted emotionally and sought revenge, trying to crush Quebec nationalism once and for all. He imposed a constitutional plan that was no more acceptable to the "No" side than to the "Yes." History would show that Trudeau wasted his victory.

Because of his actions in 1981–82, Pierre Trudeau is the true author of the Meech failure. Patriation, which had broad support in English Canada at the time, quickly boomeranged. Until 1981, Quebec had the acknowledged right to oppose any constitutional changes. Thus, the events of 1981–82 marked a turning-point in relations between the two peoples, and provoked a crisis of confidence in Quebec. René Lévesque made a prophetic declaration on 4 February 1982: "Prime Minister Trudeau is paving the way for a lot of changes that he can't even imagine."

THE 1982 CONSTITUTION:
A CRUSHING BLOW FOR QUEBEC

Quebec's minimum position since 1960 has always been that patriation must be accompanied by a clear definition of Quebec's powers in jurisdictions such as communications, education, and social affairs. Until 1976 successive Quebec governments also demanded a fairly rigid amending formula, including a right of veto for Quebec, to guarantee the province's long-term security.

Loss of the right of veto was a major setback for Quebec. Although this right was not inscribed in the BNA Act, it had nonetheless been validated by constitutional custom. Most proposals for constitutional reform over the past decades had, in fact, recommended formalizing Quebec's veto. The amending formula agreed upon in the 1982 Constitution, however, required the assent of the federal government and of seven provinces representing at least 50 percent of the population of Canada. As Georges Mathews notes: "The constitution of 1982 enables the federal government to take over provincial jurisdictions bit by bit ... as long as the anglophone majority agrees ... With the new amending formula, Quebec has *less* power than the four Atlantic provinces combined, which have less than a third of its population."[13]

At Victoria in 1971, the constitutional proposals that were eventually rejected by Quebec provided for an amending formula that required consent by the federal Parliament and the legislatures of a majority of the provinces (which must include Quebec and Ontario), two of the four western provinces, and two of the four Atlantic provinces accounting for at least 50 percent of the population of those regions. In 1981, Quebec found itself with much less than what was asked for in 1971. Trudeau's declaration in April 1982 that "Quebec had missed its chance in Victoria because it was too greedy"[14] clearly demonstrated the revenge-oriented, anti-Québécois nature of his approach.

The new constitution also failed to recognize the existence of a Quebec nation, or even to acknowledge the distinct nature of Quebec as the only province with a francophone majority. This rejection was justified in the name of the equality of the provinces, and the priority of individual rights. Yet, during the Meech debate, the Trudeauites didn't hesitate to demand that certain collective rights – such as those of native peoples or of women – take precedence over the charter.[15]

This contradictory attitude is typical, however. Throughout his rule, Trudeau sought to foster as much as possible, through legislation or constitutional protection, what might be called the multiple collective affiliations of individuals. Think, for example, of the Liberal policies favouring women, natives, the young, the disabled,[16] and so on. Trudeauites have no trouble recognizing these collective affiliations, including membership in a linguistic group, which is sanctioned and encouraged as long as it falls within one of the two official languages... The trouble starts with "national" affiliation. The Trudeauites maintain that the rights of a geographically based ethnic group should not be given the same recognition as the rights of natives or linguistic minorities. It is high time to denounce this double standard, this contradiction that is at the heart of the elucubrations of the former prime minister and his disciples. Ultimately, by denying the collective rights of the Québécois, Trudeau simply gave precedence to the collective rights of the Anglo-Canadian majority, thereby inevitably sanctioning its domination.[17]

As for the Charter of Rights, that would prove to be a veritable time bomb. While providing no help for the francophone minorities experiencing assimilation, it attacked several of the provisions of Bill 101 head-on. As we shall see in chapter 6, the charter would in fact be interpreted by federal judges in such a way as to short-circuit several of the clauses in Bill 101. Through the charter, Quebec's powers over education, language, and culture would be called into question.

Everyone but Quebec would emerge a winner from the patriation operation that was supposed to renew federalism in order to respond to Quebec's aspirations. The federal government obtained "its" Charter of Rights, the West won additional powers in the field of natural resources and "its" amending formula, the Maritime provinces obtained a firm commitment to equalization and to the principle of equal opportunities between provinces, and Ontario managed to avoid the imposition of bilingualism in Parliament and the courts, something which had existed in Quebec since the early days of confederation.[18]

FROM THE "BEAU RISQUE" TO MEECH LAKE

In 1982 and 1983 the economic crisis, which hit Quebec particularly hard, imposed a draconian austerity policy on the Parti Québécois government. The disastrous budget situation and cuts to the public sector spelled the end of the Parti Québécois' militant grass roots support, and of a good part of its electoral support as well. The election in 1984 of Brian Mulroney, who had the backing of a number of Québécois nationalists, combined with the post-referendum blues and the exhaustion of the Parti Québécois, persuaded René Lévesque to go along with the *"beau risque"* of federalism. With defeat of the federal Liberals came an atmosphere of détente in federal-provincial relations that allowed Quebec to settle certain constitutional disputes to its advantage. In constitutional matters, however, in addition to what Meech Lake would eventually contain, the Parti Québécois would go on demanding full powers over language, Quebec's exemption from the federal Charter of Rights, and more powers in the economic, social and manpower training fields.

The defeat of the Parti Québécois in December 1985 helped create a favourable climate for Meech Lake. The Parti Québécois, racked by endless internal conflicts, was in no position to resist effectively the new constitutional round for which Robert Bourassa was feverishly preparing. Although the time was right for Bourassa, who wanted to rid himself of the constitutional burden once and for all, it was unfortunately not so favourable for those promoting "the higher interests of Quebec."

The Accord: Compromise or Dirty Deal?

It was in May 1986, during a conference at Mont Gabriel, that Gil Rémillard first stated clearly the five conditions that would enable Quebec to recognize the legitimacy of the 1982 amendments to the Constitution and participate in the process of constitutional change in the future. Until then Quebec had been content with observer status at the various constitutional conferences, including those dealing with native peoples, which obviously made any agreement on this matter difficult. The main objectives in 1987 were to put an end to the *moral* exclusion that Quebec had been a victim of in 1982, to make the new constitution acceptable to the government of Quebec, and to reinforce the legitimacy of the constitution in the eyes of the Québécois.

In August and again in November 1986, the provincial premiers publicly committed themselves to settling Quebec's five demands first and postponing the other constitutional questions until a subsequent round. It seemed obvious to everyone that no progress could be made in other areas until the Quebec question had been settled.

THE JUNE 1987 ACCORD: SOME MAJOR COMPROMISES

During the negotiation process between July 1986 and 3 June 1987 when the final text of the accord was adopted, Quebec agreed to numerous modifications of its five conditions, although these were already seen as minimal. Contrary to the persistent myth circulated in English Canada that Quebec had got everything it wanted and more, and contrary to claims made by the government of Quebec when it defended the accord to its own population, in the end Quebec agreed to substantial concessions before it signed the accord.

In purely symbolic terms, Meech granted Quebec, for the first time since 1867, explicit recognition of its distinct nature. On the other hand, the chief weakness of the accord, the one that would prove to be its Achilles' heel, was the ambiguity, deliberately maintained by the politicians, as to the true consequences of this recognition. History will judge harshly those elected representatives who took refuge behind language that was inspired more by public relations than by concern for a country's future. How else can the diametrically opposed readings of English Canada and Quebec be explained? How else could the same accord symbolize so many different things to so many people?

In part, this is because, over those three long years, attempts were made to fit the accord between two stools: decentralization and centralization, or two founding nations and duality.[1] For some, Meech introduced, for the first time, recognition of Quebec's territoriality, while for others the accord's many weaknesses actually cancelled out the ostensible acceptance of Quebec's distinct nature. More than any other aspect, interpretations of the accord as supporting both duality and distinct society confirmed this unhealthy ambiguity. And it's not surprising that the accord should have suited the Quebec premier so well. Meech Lake was in a way the constitutional version of Bill 178: decentralized on the outside, centralized on the inside. What mattered was the façade and that there should be at least the appearance of special status. The problem was precisely that: it was only an appearance.

It was mainly the accord's opponents, nationalist or Trudeauite, who advanced "rational" arguments, while the pro-

Meechers appealed to the emotions, focused only rarely on content, and took their inspiration mainly from the consequences that would befall the country in the event of failure. As for the so-called nationalist circles,[2] they talked about the accord as an "unspeakable loss" in that it did not explicitly recognize what constituted Quebec's distinctness – namely its French character. The Parti Québécois saw it as proof that federalism could not be renewed, whence the need for sovereignty and the accusation that Bourassa had "sold the house for less than market value."[3]

Unconditional federalists or centralists felt that Meech would weaken the federal government and give Quebec preferential treatment the other provinces were refused, thereby hurling the country into anarchy and balkanization. This was obviously exaggerated, and mainly reflected the panic of those who couldn't swallow even an apparent recognition of Quebec's distinct nature. Here again we come back to the ambiguity of an accord that gave rise to an incalculable number of different positions. With such a vague document, each side could do with it what it wanted – and too often did so for exclusively political ends.

IMMIGRATION

Where immigration was concerned, under the terms of the Mont Gabriel declaration Quebec was to all practical purposes asking for full powers. Meech Lake granted Quebec only official constitutional recognition of the 1978 Cullen-Couture agreement,[4] a guarantee that it would receive its share of immigrants (proportionate to its share of the population of Canada), as well as the transfer of responsibility for certain services for new immigrants. On the other hand, Lowell Murray maintained that the accord clearly recognized federal supremacy in this field,[5] including responsibility for establishing the standards and goals of immigration policies according to the national interest.

By allowing any province to negotiate a Cullen-Couture kind of agreement with Ottawa, Meech refused to recognize Quebec's particular needs regarding the selection and integration of immigrants. Moreover, the federal government retained the power to modify any immigration policy unilaterally. As for the provision guaranteeing Quebec a number of immigrants in proportion to its share of the population of Canada, with the right to exceed that figure by 5 percent for demographic reasons, that provision was also granted to the other provinces in that they could negotiate agreements similar to Quebec's.

FEDERAL SPENDING POWER

On the matter of federal spending power, Rémillard had asked that agreement of the provinces be required to modify the formula for equalization payments and transfer payments. On that score, he obtained nothing. For a *distinct society*, however, absolute protection against any federal intrusion would have been an essential tool to achieve the national destiny of Quebec. In point of fact, the true scope of the article on spending powers for the provinces was very limited. Five conditions had to be respected in order for a province to withdraw from a program and receive financial compensation: it must be national; shared-cost; set up after the accord came into effect; in a field of exclusively provincial jurisdiction; and the provinces would receive "fair financial compensation" only on condition that they implement a program or an initiative "compatible with national objectives." In short, the federal government's power remained intact.

Contrary to the 1867 constitution, which said nothing about federal spending power, Meech for the first time recognized federal government spending power in provincial jurisdictions, but it also allowed Ottawa to decide the broad direction for all programs. And as usual, in case of disagreement the Supreme Court was given responsibility for deciding whether a provincial program was acceptable.

Ottawa thus could have watered down or taken issue with some of Quebec's exclusive legislative spheres. Consequently, and perhaps more than any others, such a provision ran counter to the very notion of a distinct society. For the first time in history, Robert Bourassa agreed to allow the federal government to impose conditions inside provincial jurisdictions. This was a major concession, if we consider as well that, as a federal representative confirmed, "the first ministers' intention during their negotiations had been to discourage the right to withdraw"[6] by imposing parameters defined exclusively by the federal government. According to Professors Andrée Lajoie and Jacques Frémont: "What may appear at first sight to be a federal government concession to Quebec and the provinces will be revealed, after more detailed examination, as a major victory for Ottawa, who will thereby finally be able to do what it has been attempting for years, namely to acquire the constitutional authority to invest and, to all practical purposes, control every area of exclusively provincial jurisdiction."[7]

Bourassa agreed, then, to allow Ottawa to enshrine in the constitution a practice that already existed, but that the provinces had often opposed. What in the past had been a litigious practice by the federal government would become a wholly legitimate act. Through his agreement, the Quebec premier was risking transfers of power that could eventually put Quebec at a disadvantage. This arrangement, then, was a clear retreat. Hadn't the Quebec Liberal Party itself, in 1985, demanded nothing less than a right of veto over federal spending powers? Once again, Bourassa had chosen to reduce the impact of the distinct society in exchange for a document that would finally bring him constitutional peace.

THE RIGHT OF VETO

Recognition of the right of veto was one of Quebec's fundamental conditions. Quebec had lost this historic right, which had been used most notably in 1965 and 1971, at the time of patriation in 1981. In Edmonton in August 1988, Bourassa proposed that any province representing 25 percent or more of the population should have a right of veto, and that this should be an acquired right, even if the population should drop below the 25 percent mark. A wise precaution for Quebec, whose declining population today represents only 26 percent of Canada as a whole. The June 1987 agreement did not restore Quebec's full right of veto, insofar as the rule of unanimity was applied to certain very limited items: powers of the Senate and the method for selecting Senators, the Supreme Court, the principle of proportional representation in the House of Commons, and the creation of new provinces. This was far from the overall right of veto demanded by Quebec, since in most cases the 1982 amending formula would have still applied. It was enough that the parliaments of Canada and of seven provinces representing at least 50 percent of the Canadian population give their consent. As Brian Mulroney put it so well, "it is important to remember from the outset that the Meech Lake Accord does not amend the general formula for constitutional change."[8]

Moreover, by undertaking on 9 June 1990 to implement an elected and more "equitable" Senate, Bourassa was sacrificing the only real advantage he had managed to extract from the Meech Lake Accord, that is, a right of veto over any extensive change to federal institutions. By so doing he let go of Quebec's only weapon against the creation of a Senate that, beyond any doubt, would not have corresponded with the province's interests. In fact this element figured heavily in Manitoba's decision to ratify the accord.

As for the Supreme Court, the accord enshrined the already accepted practice of appointing three judges from Quebec. As far as participation in selecting judges was concerned, a kind of double veto would prevail. Quebec would draw up a list of potential candidates and the federal government would make its choice from that list, on the condition that it include at least one acceptable candidate.

The real problem, however, was much broader: that of the society one chooses and the mechanisms whereby it assumes its legitimacy. By refusing to clarify the notion of a distinct society, and by giving the Supreme Court the job of defining its exact meaning, the accord placed the future of Quebec squarely in the hands of nine non-elected judges, six of them from English-speaking provinces. Thus Meech Lake continued the process of eroding parliamentary sovereignty already set in motion by the promulgation of the Canadian Charter of Rights and Freedoms. To a large extent since 1982, on questions that would be fundamental for the future of any nation, the Supreme Court has been governing far more than our elected members have, rendering decisions clearly more political than legal. When he signed Meech, what Bourassa was sanctioning was the poisoned gift left to us by Trudeau.

THE DISTINCT SOCIETY

That politicians on both sides have chosen to maintain great confusion about the distinct society has been due above all to the difficulty of selling that concept both to Quebec and to English Canada. Two different arguments were needed that, in the end, could only contradict each other publicly. Thus, to avoid alarming the Québécois, who were only too happy to see that they had been "accepted" by the rest of the country, pro-Meech politicians deliberately omitted mentioning the paragraphs about duality and the confirmation of the respective powers of the federal government and the provinces in this area, which in fact would have watered down the impact of the distinct society. The Trudeauite opponents, however, had no qualms about making political capital on the back of an accord that was depicted as an unacceptable concession to Quebec that left the English-speaking provinces out in the cold.

It is not surprising, then, that the accord should have been the subject of contradictory statements. Take Mulroney, who as early as 20 August 1987 was confirming that the distinct society clause had no legal impact: "You can be certain that there is nothing in the Meech Lake Accord that in any way diminishes the rights of women or anyone else."[9] Or Murray, who noted that the distinct society would operate "in harmony" with Article 1 of the Charter.[10] Or Rémillard, who changed his mind on the matter just about every day. Or again, Bourassa himself, who now saw no fewer than three levels of protection for the French language in Quebec: Article 1 of the Charter, the distinct society clause, and the notwithstanding clause.[11]

The distinct society clause is not in the accord by chance. Why would the federal government have taken the initiative to give Bourassa, who only wanted it to be included in the preamble, more than he requested? Essentially, it was because its role would be far more political than legal. By creating the illusion that it could lead to increased powers for Quebec, the distinct society provision concealed the main shortcoming of the accord, which was precisely that it established no new division of powers. Had the clause been obtained on the condition that the accord would not derogate from the powers, rights, or privileges of parliaments or governments, including those pertaining to language? What can be said about a Quebec premier who accepted such a deal, thereby abandoning the demands made by his predecessors? How could such a constitution have been signed when it left unsettled, as Claude Ryan himself recognized, the whole question of the division of powers?[12]

Beyond the petty squabbles and the contradictory analyses, the distinct society provision was meaningless because it granted no new powers to Quebec, did not refer to the French language and culture as being essential components of that distinctness, and would have been rendered nul and void by the other measures contained in the accord. Just as Trudeau had done with his charter, there was an attempt to make us believe that the survival of a people was a legal matter, whereas it was actually an essentially political problem. You don't negotiate a nation's future by hiding behind legal jargon or by refusing to negotiate a new division of powers.

In addition, when Bourassa declared that "the constitution should be interpreted according to this article [distinct society], which is much stronger than a mention in the preamble,"[13] he was making sure no attention was drawn to the danger inherent in the interpretation of duality. Moreover, instead of simply giving Quebec exclusive jurisdiction over linguistic matters, Meech granted the federal and provincial governments the role of protecting Canadian duality. If both the Meech Lake Accord and Bill 101 had been in effect, Quebec would probably have become the only state in the world to be simultaneously bilingual and unilingual! In an attempt to conceal this aberration, a false polemic was launched that focused on the charter's precedence over the distinct society provision, when the real problem lay elsewhere. Meanwhile, Bourassa was swearing up and down that this clause finally guaranteed Quebec "absolute linguistic security."

After the Supreme Court ruling of 15 December 1988, José Woehrling, a professor of law at Université de Montréal, concluded that the true problem – the one that was liable to cost Quebec the most – was that duality would inevitably take precedence over the distinct society:

Had the Meech Lake Accord been in effect, it would not have improved the case of Bill 101 before the Supreme Court. On the contrary, the "role" of protecting Canadian duality that is assigned to Quebec could very probably be considered as another argument to justify invalidating the provisions that prohibit English signs.[14]

Most specialists who had testified before the Quebec parliamentary commission had confirmed the limitations of the distinct society provision:

The opinion of the majority of Québécois experts is that the consequences of the distinct society clause are obviously restricted by the principle of Canadian duality (a fundamental characteristic), as inscribed in the Meech Lake Accord, and by certain prescriptions of the Charter of Rights and Freedoms. In short, in their opinion it will be difficult to make French prevail over the other languages in Quebec by relying on this article.[15]

And so Meech tried to reconcile a number of irreconcilable notions: centralization and decentralization, duality and multiculturalism, territoriality and non-territoriality, etc. He who grasps at too much loses all, and trying to describe a country that was defined by its refusal to define itself brought the risk of a legal quagmire from which only the lawyers would have benefitted. But was there really any ambiguity? Or were we dealing with a clause whose interpretation was actually far more precise than the politicians would have liked it to appear? To answer this question, we must obviously look at the entire accord, the better to judge its impact on the distinct society.

The notion of duality in the accord refers to the existence of French-speaking and English-speaking Canadians. The concept of duality is defined therefore "in terms of the language used, and not in terms of socio-cultural groups defined essentially in terms of mother tongue."[16] In fact Meech breaks little new ground in this regard because the equality of the two languages, not of the groups that speak them, was already contained in article 16 of the Canadian Charter of Rights and Freedoms. The 20 April 1987 version of the clause – the one Bourassa allowed to slip between his fingers – would have enshrined a territorial and collectivist vision by referring to the existence of an English Canada and a French Canada. Between April and June 1987, however, this version was replaced by one that was non-territorial and hence more individualist. It could even be said that the "Meech" duality is a perfect match for the "Trudeau" duality, which erased biculturalism from the picture, replacing it with bilingualism in the 1969 Official Languages Act, thereby refusing to recognize Quebec as the national homeland of Canada's francophone majority. But none of this occurred by chance. The Trudeauite influence can be seen even in the Mulroney government's new official languages law, which grants to linguistic minorities only collective rights to be guaranteed by Ottawa.[17]

With Meech, Quebec would soon have found itself caught between two potentially contradictory interpretations – of multiculturalism (article 27 of the charter) and the distinct society; the latter could also conflict with the interpretation of duality. It is unnecessary to add that such legal and semantic confusion between collective and individual rights would have been very dangerous for Quebec. And was it not common sense that led Jacques Parizeau to say:

If it [the distinct society] really has any significance, it will always in some way be in conflict with the letter and the spirit of the Charter of Rights, simply because that clause aims at protecting and promoting the rights and the interests of a society. The omnipresent opposition between individual and collective rights will quickly reappear.[18]

In any event, with or without duality *à la* Meech, Quebec is still bound by the Canadian constitution and by its provisions regarding multiculturalism and duality. And as if all this confusion weren't enough, enshrining in the constitution Quebec's duty to protect and promote its anglophone minority, whose presence was a component of duality and – let's not forget it – of its own distinctness, would have been a major obstacle to the preservation and development of a society that wanted to be more and more French.

Thus the acknowledgment of Quebec's distinct nature, which seemed unreserved in Rémillard's presentation at Mont Gabriel, was considerably diminished by constitutional protection of linguistic duality and the anglo-Quebec minority, as well as by the explicit admission that Quebec would not benefit from any new power (or from powers different from those of the other provinces) to promote its specificity. If it was to have any meaning whatever, the distinct society clause would have had to grant broader powers and responsibilities to the government of Quebec, so that it would be in a position to orient and develop this distinct character. Rémillard's claim that the distinct society was "a genuine declaration of power" rather than a simple clause with which to interpret the constitution was therefore unfounded.

By signing the accord, Bourassa, as could have been expected, once again refused to make a choice. Except that this time the choice was crucial for the future of Quebec. It was clear and simple. Either Quebec would opt for duality, that is bilingualism, or it would choose to be a genuinely distinct, that is an essentially French society. Under such circumstances, it's impossible not to choose. Any decision would inevitably cause the pendulum to swing in one direction or the other. As far as Meech was concerned, in the June 1987 version, Bourassa would have actually established Quebec as the only province that was constitutionally bilingual. Only the notwithstanding clause in the Charter of Rights would have let Quebec out of the ensuing obligations. What reason was there then to sign an accord that would have required Quebec to govern by means of a notwithstanding clause? Unless it was, once again, to buy a temporary peace.

THE "NEW ACCORD" OF 9 JUNE 1990[19]

If the June 1987 accord was seriously tainted, what can be said about the additional concessions that the premier of Quebec agreed to following the June 1990 constitutional marathon? Even if it appeared that no amendment had been made to Meech Lake, the major retreats contained in the political agreement signed on 9 June made Bourassa's triumphant attitude indecent. In the short term, the concessions had been skilfully doctored, but in the longer term they would water down the accord even more and weaken Quebec's position in the constitutional negotiations to which it had committed itself.

When it returned from Ottawa, the Quebec delegation spared no effort to convince us that the legal opinion appended to the accord was just a piece of paper without much importance. In English Canada, however, many experts and politicians felt that the opinion represented a significant gain for those opposed to the distinct society. Gary Filmon and Clyde Wells would have refused to sign the accord, in fact, if the opinion had not been appended to the political agreement. On CBC-TV last 11 June, Montreal lawyer Julius Grey, a strong defender of anglophone rights, rejoiced at how this weakened the concept of the distinct society. He also stated his conviction, based on several legal precedents, that the opinion would eventually be taken into consideration by the Supreme Court.

Indeed, it's hard to imagine that, when the time came to interpret laws passed on the basis of the distinct society clause, the Supreme Court would have been able to ignore this opinion which the first ministers had thought advisable to append to their political agreement. It was absurd to claim that the judges wouldn't have looked to this opinion for clarification about what the legislators wanted.

By confirming unambiguously that the distinct society could not be dissociated from Canadian duality, this opinion threw the doors open not only to confusion, for the notions are potentially contradictory, but also to the possibility that duality would take precedence. It confirmed as well that "the clause did not create any new legislative powers for Parliament or for any of the provincial legislatures." As we have seen, that was what Mulroney and Bourassa had been telling English Canada for months to get the accord passed. In Quebec, however, Bourassa had maintained more than once that the distinct society clause would expand Quebec's powers and its room to manoeuvre.

As for Senate reform, the Quebec premier declared that he had consented only to some vague, non-restrictive "parameters," and that in any case Quebec still had its veto. The reality was unfortunately not so simple. Here too, Filmon, Wells,

Carstairs, Doer, Getty and others thought they had won a victory.

A constitutional conference on the Senate was to be held before the end of 1990. The "parameters" for reform would be an elected Senate with greater representation for the less populous provinces and real powers that would take greater account of the interests of those provinces and reflect Canadian duality. Even if it was hard to oppose reform of that archaic institution, and even if its representation would very likely remain intact, Quebec would have seen its political power inside the Canadian federation seriously compromised if it had agreed to a reform based on the principles contained in the agreement of 9 June. In fact, a Senate that gave more powers to the less populous provinces would have weakened the relative position of Quebec. Furthermore, as columnist Jeffrey Simpson confirmed, an elected and thus more legitimate senate, with real powers, would inevitably have strengthened federal authority at Quebec's expense.[20] The American example shows that the existence of two elected legislative chambers at the federal level increases the political weight of the central state.

By a strange coincidence, the French version of the agreement on the Senate matched the demands of the government of Quebec much more closely than did the English version. The three *paramètres* of reform were *objectives* in the English text. But there was another subtle but important difference between the two versions. Although the three parameters were couched in the conditional in both languages, the English text introduced the reform with an affirmative formula (the future tense): "Proposals for senate reform that *will* give effect to the following objectives." The French text presented reform in the conditional: "dont la base *serait* les paramètres suivants."

To the delight of his English-Canadian counterparts, Bourassa had finally made a solemn promise, moral as well as political, to carry out a reform based on precise objectives. In English Canada, expectations were high. The political cost of attempting to use the veto to override the process would have been astronomical. At the very least, any future demands by Quebec would have been indefinitely postponed, and the eventual "Canada clause" especially hard for Quebec to swallow.

On 9 June, the first ministers had agreed to include in a preamble to the constitution a definition of the country's fundamental characteristics. This was a major concession to the recalcitrant provinces. Even if it were "compatible with the constitution," the "Canada clause" would have considerably lessened the already seriously compromised impact of the distinct society clause by adding elements – multiculturalism and duality, for example – that would influence judicial interpretation when it came time to settle constitutional disputes. And if by some misfortune it had reasserted the rights of all Canadian citizens to equality and the equality of the provinces, the new preamble would have undermined the notion of "collective rights" underlying the distinct society. Taking into account the real and potential modifications concerning the distinct society which the Quebec government had already agreed to, Bourassa's threat to leave the conference on the night of Thursday, 7 June, seemed more theatrical than a rare show of decisiveness.

As the Canada clause was subject to the amending formula which required "seven provinces representing at least 50 percent of the population," Quebec would moreover have found itself in a weaker position for negotiating its contents, especially since several of the English-Canadian premiers were already vowing to seize this opportunity to repay Quebec in kind. Those who still doubt the relevance or the constitutional significance of a preamble must not forget that it was the preamble to article 91 of the BNA Act that for several decades allowed the federal government to increase its legislative powers in the name of "peace, order and good government."

The process for adopting the Meech Lake Accord also contributed to weakening Quebec's position during the coming rounds. English Canada finally agreed to Meech, largely thanks

to the creation of apocalyptic scenarios about Quebec's separation and the subsequent dissolution of Canada. If Wells and
Filmon finally seemed to give in on the night of 9 June 1990,
it was not only because of concessions by Quebec but also
because the two premiers had been convinced that they would
have to bear responsibility for the break-up of Canada.

When Bourassa, no doubt a little uncomfortable about the
booty he had obtained in Ottawa, talked about demanding more
powers over manpower and communications during a second
round,[21] he was dreaming. The anglophone premiers and opinion leaders felt that they had already been very "generous"
towards Quebec. Expectations for the upcoming constitutional
rounds were therefore exceptionally high. Now it was Quebec's
turn to be generous. There is no doubt that the second round
would have been exclusively English Canada's, and Quebec
would have had to be content with "playing defence," as one
of the premier's chief advisers put it. Moreover, as Lise Bissonnette emphasized in *Le Devoir*:

The *minimum* was obviously becoming English Canada's ultimate concession to the eternally rebellious province. It would never be a
springboard towards broader powers for Quebec. Really, we've just
had a narrow escape. If the Québécois have never intended to be
satisfied with minimal conditions for participating in the federation –
and who'd want that! – they shouldn't complain about the refusal
they've just been handed.[22]

It is highly revealing that criticisms of the accord by Québécois nationalists have been corroborated by a considerable
portion of the English-Canadian intelligentsia who had supported Meech Lake. The accord would have guaranteed Quebec's adherence to the Canadian constitution in return for some
rather minor changes, contributed to national unity, and
reduced tensions within the Canadian federation. This opinion
was expressed by Gordon Roberston, a former senior official

close to the Trudeau government. In a detailed analysis entitled "The Five Myths Of Meech Lake," Robertson concluded that the distinct society clause conferred no new powers on Quebec and could not be used in opposition to the Charter of Rights; gave constitutional legitimacy to federal programs in areas of exclusively provincial jurisdiction that would have been subject only to provincial variations compatible with federal government objectives; and finally, did not in any way reflect the existence of two nations within Canada.[23]

Throughout this affair the current government of Quebec, to avoid having to deal with the consequences of failure, seemed to be trying to reach a political agreement with English Canada at any price, to the detriment of the so-called higher interests of Quebec. If the Québécois chose to celebrate instead of weeping on 24 June 1990, it's not hard to understand why. The *minimum* demanded at Mont Gabriel in 1986 became the *compromise* of Meech Lake in 1987, which in turn was transformed into *capitulation* in Ottawa on 9 June 1990. Under the circumstances, should we trust that same group of men and women to redefine the political status of Quebec? I'll come back to that.

From Mayhem to Psychodrama

NATIONAL RECONCILIATION

As soon as Brian Mulroney came to power he delivered his famous speech at Sept-Iles in which he undertook to reintegrate Quebec into the constitutional family "with honour and enthusiasm." For Quebec, these few words, which had been whispered to the prime minister by Lucien Bouchard, signified that Ottawa finally intended to deliver the goods Pierre Trudeau had promised back in 1980.

In contrast, if we look at the constitutional proposals in the Quebec Liberals' 1985 electoral program, things looked rather grim; Robert Bourassa already seemed prepared to negotiate at a loss. Moreover, the demands clearly fell short of those made by the Lévesque government. Of the twenty-two conditions submitted by the Parti Québécois, Bourassa had retained only five.

It's true that after two decades of confrontations between Ottawa and Quebec, Mulroney could take advantage of circumstances that encouraged national reconciliation. Good will was bursting out all over. Ed Broadbent's NDP was willing to go along. Briefly thumbing their noses at the Trudeauites in the party, John Turner's Liberals undertook to recognize the distinct nature of Quebec.[1] As for the Parti Québécois under Pierre Marc Johnson, it intended to make the spectre of sovereignty quietly disappear.

Ottawa, in the meantime, was preparing the way by moving quickly on a series of concessions to Quebec.[2] Even David

Peterson was saying that he understood the "special and unique nature of Quebec and its need for specific protection,"[3] and was promising to revive the historic Ottawa-Toronto-Quebec axis. Yet the same Peterson was fiercely opposed to any special status for Quebec until the ratification of Meech in June 1987, and he used his election campaign to threaten to drag Quebec into court unless it played according to established constitutional rules.

To the delight of Bourassa, the provincial premiers managed to agree at Edmonton, in August 1986, that the next round of negotiations would be exclusively Quebec's. (Their shopping lists would come later, once this little commitment had been forgotten.) On the basis of Quebec's five conditions, the real work began – the work of the civil servants, lawyers, consultants, and committees.

Although some observers, such as Daniel Latouche,[4] saw Bourassa as a "skilful negotiator" who had wrung concessions from Ottawa from start to finish, it seems in fact that by opting for the minimum, in spite of a situation that put him in a strong position, he ended by being content with very little.

Bourassa, a pseudo-democrat, had even had the audacity to establish a parliamentary commission which had only thirty-five hours to study such an important document. Both the Parti Québécois and the Quebec Liberals had brought out their big guns – Jacques-Yvan Morin, Solange Chaput-Rolland, Gérald Beaudoin, Léon Dion, Jacques Parizeau, etc. Nationalist criticisms, on the other hand – which would be compared with those of the centralizing federalists to the extent that they were both considered to be completely out of step – would have little impact or audience in the end.

If Mulroney could give the impression on 4 June 1987 that he had finally kept the promise made by Trudeau in May 1980, if English Canada appeared to have said "Yes" to a distinct Quebec, if Québécois editorial writers were singing the praises of the accord, and if Bourassa could declare Canada to be "one of the best countries in the world," saying he could now "go home with his head high," it was above all because everything had been done with the greatest discretion, and with the greatest indifference toward a public who were largely mystified by the legal jargon of the accord, and about its consequences.

In the euphoria of the moment, the distinct society which Quebec Liberals hoped to see in the preamble found itself "promoted" to the rank of an interpretative rule. Too busy rejoicing, few Québécois analysts paid any attention at the time to the other interpretative rule – i.e. duality – whose impact would make itself felt in December 1988 when the Supreme Court handed down its judgment on unilingual signs. In retrospect, Bourassa's claim that the French language in Quebec was now protected "in an absolute fashion"[5] seems absurd.

There were boasts in the Quebec media that the accord contained substantial gains for Quebec, even the acquisition of additional room for manoeuvre that would lead to new powers. Nationalists who dared to oppose Meech were booed and denounced as "spoilsports," as "poor losers," or as miserable "defeatists." *Le Soleil* even went so far as to ask in a headline, "What If the PQ Were Superfluous?"[6] while Michel Vastel openly poked fun at Johnson.[7] However, a number of nationalists, although they were crying in the desert, had already begun to point out the principal gaps in the accord. And it is important to remember that, although he received little coverage, Johnson nonetheless gave Premier Bourassa a good fight. Even Gilles Rhéaume made what sounded at the time like a completely harebrained prediction that Meech would inevitably lead to a revival of the independentist movement.[8]

English Canadians opposed to the distinct society were seen as fanatics and clearly in the minority. It was claimed that nationalists were outmoded and that the Trudeauites were finally dead and buried. It's too bad that so little attention was paid to the very different way that English Canada was reading the accord. Too bad that not enough was made of the anglo-phone premiers' treating Bourassa as "one of the boys." Too bad no one listened to Turner who, in a rare moment of lucidity, said that "the ambiguity in the Meech Lake agreement which led some to believe that we're going back to the concept of two nations has been corrected."[9] And too bad that the report of the Special Joint Committee of the Senate and the House of Commons on the constitutional agreement, in which we find a false and contemptuous vision of Quebec, wasn't read carefully. One of its rare readers said that it gave the impression of a Quebec that was clinging, prickly, and expensive.[10]

It certainly looks as if Bourassa preferred not to give these "party-poopers" too much time for in-depth analyses, because he suspended both the rules and parliamentary work so the National Assembly could ratify the accord before adjourning. In the face of an English Canada that was already turning rebellious, Bourassa preferred to send a clear message so they could move on to something else as quickly as possible. Already, before the signatures of the English-Canadian premiers were even dry, he felt he must refuse any change or amendment. The honeymoon was a short one.

The breach was there, however, and it was growing inexorably while Bourassa and Gil Rémillard were boasting about having made "enormous gains" and Mulroney and Lowell Murray were doing their best to tell English Canada the very opposite. "Who is telling the truth?" Johnson asked the premier. Bourassa might as well have answered, "We'll ask the Supreme Court."

During the summer of 1987, a Special Joint Committee of the Senate and the House of Commons showed that there was strong opposition to the accord in English Canada and that many people were demanding that it be re-opened. This was when the pro-Meech side left the field of rational argument and began to talk only in terms of the possibly disastrous consequences of failure. This threat of constitutional apocalypse was strangely reminiscent of the 1980 referendum, and at the same time demonstrated a sad inability to defend the accord on its merits.

Quebec's support for free trade during the November 1988 federal election campaign, and the granting of the F-18 maintenance contract to Bombardier instead of to a Manitoba firm, would provide English Canada with the first in a long series of pretexts for opposing an accord that it could not, in any case, accept. The reasons included senate reform, women, anglo-Quebeckers, francophones outside Quebec, ethnic groups, the list goes on ... Just remember Manitoba premier Howard Pawley warning Bourassa that Meech could be in for a serious beating because of his support for free trade, while at the same time he acknowledged that most members of his legislature, from all three parties, were fiercely opposed to the accord[11] and that there was "an anti-Quebec backlash" in the West.[12]

In spite of the storm that was brewing, by June 1988 only British Columbia, Newfoundland, New Brunswick, and Manitoba had not yet ratified the accord. On the other hand – and it was here that everything would be played out – opposition in English-Canadian public opinion was growing stronger.

THE EROSION OF SUPPORT

Impatient and impenitent as ever, Trudeau released the first salvo against the accord before the final version was written.[13] In his eagerness to cause the blind to see and the halt to walk, what the former prime minister actually accomplished was to make them deaf to Quebec's demands.

Summoning the troops, Trudeau cracked open the door of the Canadian closet, from which an alarming number of skeletons would finally emerge. And what would better awaken the dead than some old ideas everyone had thought buried – such as his famous vision of the country, unchanged after all these years:

Since 1982, Canada had its constitution, including a Charter which was binding on the provinces as well as the federal government. From then on, the advantage was on the Canadian government's side; it no longer had anything very urgent to seek from the provinces; it was they who had become the supplicants. Henceforth "Canada's constitutional evolution" could have come about without preconditions and without blackmail, on the basis of give and take among equals ... With the assurance of a creative equilibrium between the provinces and the central government, the federation was set to last a thousand years![14]

In Trudeau's Reich, equality meant a balance of power between forces that clearly favoured the central government, to the particular detriment of the only province that really needed special powers. This was clear to Clyde Wells, Sharon Carstairs, Gary Filmon, and company, who were now hastening to dismiss the promise by the provincial premiers "to give priority to examining Quebec's conditions and not to tie the outcome of such an examination to that of their own constitutional powers."[15]

Enjoying a fairly active retirement, Trudeau kept intervening, whether it was through a speech to the Senate Plenary Committee urging the English provinces to ask the Supreme Court for a verdict on the legal meaning of the distinct society, or by bringing out two books in less than two years. When he accused Mulroney of buying peace at any price, Trudeau pretended to forget the notwithstanding clause which he himself had offered to the western provinces in exchange for ratification of the 1982 constitution. That clause, in fact, would turn out to be Quebec's only genuine instrument of power.

While the old man was cutting loose, the real leader of the federal Liberals, who had been opposed to the April 1987 agreement, finally decided to support it, probably to hold on to an already shaky electoral base in Quebec. The fine unanimity within the federal Liberals wouldn't last long, however.

Aside from the hesitations openly expressed by Peterson's Liberals, and the election of Frank McKenna in New Brunswick, the moment of truth would come during the vote on the accord in the House of Commons on 26 October 1987. More than one-quarter of the Liberal caucus voted against, and the wind began to turn definitively in the old guard's favour. Turning their backs on the official party line, the Liberal senators, most of them Trudeau appointments, also refused to ratify the accord.

Laying the ground for the return of "the little guy from Shawinigan," the family squabble would soon deteriorate into a genuine *putsch*. This not particularly brilliant page in the history of the federal Liberals would result in a party devoted almost exclusively to English Canada's interests. And what can be said about the anti-Meech crusade undertaken by Liberals coast-to-coast (aside from Quebec, of course)? Or about Sharon Carstairs, Clyde Wells, and Frank McKenna who, carried along on the Trudeau wave, delighted in giving Quebec lessons in liberalism while one of their number was preparing to repudiate the signature of his predecessor?

As Quebec had changed profoundly in the past ten years, the impact in the province would be very different from that of 1980. This time, the Trudeauite Liberal current would contribute to the rise of sovereignism in Quebec. It goes without saying that anti-Meech scheming would be an important factor in Turner's departure. He would be unable to convince his caucus, unconvinced as he was himself about the accord's validity.

Nor could the NDP escape the Meech whirlwind. Behind the façade of Broadbent's unshakeable support was a party deeply divided on the question. Feeding the momentum that was running contrary to the accord, the NDP under Audrey McLaughlin would ask for major amendments, though it had approved the original text. Consistent, at least in appearance, McLaughlin had publicly opposed the accord since her election to the House of Commons in July 1987. I say in appearance, considering that she had the audacity, the day after the failure of Meech, to recognize the inevitability of a new, sovereignty-association type of agreement between Quebec and Canada – another proof that Quebec's distinct character presents no problems to anyone in English Canada as long as it is stripped of meaning or exists *outside of* federation. Like a number of English Canadians, she would be unwilling to show the same determination to defend the distinct society of the Québécois as she did that of the Iroquois during the Oka crisis.

Still, during the first days of the accord English Canada seemed ready to accept the apparently definitive defeat of the Trudeauite vision. A Goldfarb poll revealed that the majority of English-speaking Canadians approved of the Meech Lake Accord.[16] But this was based on deceptive appearances and would very quickly be refuted. Already, long before rushing to the extraordinary pretext that Bill 178 would provide, English Canada was trying to express its opposition to an accord that recognized, so it was said, the distinct nature of Quebec. Those Québécois who read only *The Globe and Mail* thought they were dreaming at the paper's happiness that Quebec was to be fully reinstated in Confederation. As for the editorial writers of most large English-Canadian dailies, they denounced an accord they felt had been bought for much too high a price. The prime minister was enjoined to take his time so that a "good" accord could be ratified. Is it necessary to recall that English Canada hadn't shown the same scruples during the constitutional negotiations in 1981-82?

In spite of everything, Meech remained afloat for almost a year. But by mid-May 1988, serious disintegration was setting in. Cracks were appearing on all sides in the ranks of the federal Liberals and the NDP. McKenna, elected in October 1987 with fifty-eight out of fifty-eight seats, was demanding supplementary protection for the Acadians and repeal of the right to opt out of federal programs. Gary Filmon, heading a newly elected minority government in Manitoba, declared "that the 1987 agreement was low on his list of priorities."[17] Carstairs refused to sign if the charter did not take absolute precedence over the distinct society clause. Gary Doer repudiated the position of his predecessor, Pawley. The Northwest Territories and the Yukon feared that the unanimous approval required in the accord for creating new provinces would prevent them from ever obtaining provincial status. Francophones outside Quebec demanded that all legislatures have responsibility for promoting duality, and natives wanted their rights to be enshrined then and there.

Through all of this, McKenna's role was obviously crucial but not decisive. He played a leading part as the first provincial premier to reject the Meech Lake Accord. Descended from Loyalist and rather conservative stock, McKenna intended to persuade the other premiers to re-open the accord. But it was the political McKenna, the one with federal ambitions, who had the edge in front of the CBC cameras and mikes when he rallied at the last minute. It was all in the interest of playing the great unifier and the saviour *in extremis* of Canadian unity.

Manitoba, in the meantime, was champing at the bit. Filmon was caught in an utterly untenable position opposite Carstairs, who refused any compromise. But had Filmon not committed himself in November 1988 to getting the accord ratified as quickly as possible?[18] Few will remember his outburst against Trudeau, whom he had accused of "dividing the country with his constitutional manacles," or his profession of faith in the accord, even if it meant making changes once it had been ratified.[19] While such rashness could not be maintained in the face of an all too real threat of losing power, it's hard to explain how he could have defended the accord in a province where anti-francophone feelings and an obsessive fear of Quebec and Ontario go back a long way.

It was when Wells came to power that the final blow was dealt to an accord that was already clinically dead. Less than twelve hours after his election, he was already promising to rescind the Peckford government's approval. If the ensuing war of attrition between St John's, Ottawa, and Quebec was vaguely reminiscent of the Trudeau-Lévesque era, it still served only to stir up passions in English Canada. Like Trudeau, who was irreparably disconnected from the reality of Quebec, Wells would display obvious ignorance of *la belle province*. And he was another who told English Canada exactly what it wanted to hear: that Quebec was a province like the others, that the distinct society clause would enable us to oppress our anglophones,[20] etc.

Throwing oil on the flames, Quebec's use of the notwithstanding clause and promulgation of Bill 178 marked a turning-point in English-Canadian public opinion. For politicians, both offered an unhoped-for pretext for once again bringing out the bugbear of the distinct society. With Alberta punishing Léo Piquette for having dared to express himself in French in the provincial legislature, Manitoba continuing with attempts to muzzle its francophone minority, Saskatchewan and Alberta confirming their unilingual English status, and British Columbia having just a handful of French schools, there was no reluctance to make a public outcry. And it was Filmon, premier of the historically most anti-francophone province in the country, who was the first to invoke Bill 178 to justify reversing his stand on Meech.

THE CONSEQUENCES OF EROSION

By subordinating everything to the obsessive quest for ratification of the accord, and by avoiding confrontation with Ottawa at all costs, Bourassa chose a strategy that would be costly for Quebec.[21] Moreover, by breaking with the traditional approach which consisted of claiming broader powers for Quebec, the premier had compromised himself from the outset. In a major negotiation, who could boast of having asked for the minimum? And when even that minimum is adrift in total ambiguity, is it surprising if divergent interpretations eventually lead to grave conflicts? Not to mention that by leaving himself open to the rejection of minimum demands, Bourassa was mining the ground for Quebec federalists. For if Mulroney's strategy here had been highly questionable, Bourassa's was frankly disastrous.

The Quebec premier then found himself trapped by his own strategy and faced with the deep opposition taking shape in English Canada. In Quebec, where his popularity was declining, Bourassa initiated a slide within his caucus toward a nationalism much closer to that of the Parti Québécois. During the September 1989 election campaign the Liberals' discourse and symbols would be "adjusted" to the mood of the Québécois. It was then that the Quebec Liberals incorporated a huge fleur-de-lys into its new "blue as the sky" logo, making it very tricky to differentiate Liberal from Parti Québécois posters. Bourassa also seemed to enjoy talking about "l'État du Québec," an expression made famous in the past by Jean Lesage. His attitude, obviously, was not disinterested. In Quebec, since the wind had turned against Meech Lake in English Canada, "nationalism" as a political platform was becoming both credible and profitable. Especially because, since the resignation of three anglophone cabinet ministers in the wake of Bill 178 and the defection of part of its English-speaking supporters, the Quebec Liberals realized that they could now afford the luxury of being more nationalist – in words at least – without the risk of too many consequences.

After all, for the first time in history the threat that the country would break up was coming not from Quebec but from English Canada, which was refusing to recognize Quebec's distinctness. The Sault-Ste-Marie episode allowed Quebec a chance to see through the smoke-screen of English Canada's indignation about Bill 178. The Québécois realized that English Canada was still fundamentally incapable of accepting Quebec's difference inside Canada. They felt the rejection that emanated not only from the Association for the Protection of English in Canada (APEC) but also from Filmon, Wells, and the majority of English Canadians. The wave of English unilingualism and the subsequent rise of sovereignism in Quebec were the result of an understanding of what was really at stake.

There is no doubt that APEC, with its comparisons between the French language and AIDS, was a relatively marginal phenomenon. However, *pace* a number of anglophones, the Québécois realized that this epiphenomenon was only one of many symptoms of a country that was, quite simply, no longer viable for them. The dazzling rise of the sovereignist option in the almost weekly opinion polls which punctuated and in part dictated the course of events attests to that.

That rise was steady and swift. In November 1989, 50 percent of Québécois were still hoping to remain in Canada, even after the failure of Meech (Sorecom). In contrast, IQOP reported in March 1990 that 67.5 percent of Québécois would now reply "Yes" to the 1980 referendum question. After ten years on the shelf, nationalism was acceptable once again. In a survey conducted in April 1990, *l'Actualité*[22] drew a portrait of a society that had reached a successful outcome after 30 years of national affirmation, but had been deeply wounded by English Canada's reaction to Meech Lake. Sixty-five percent of the Québécois questioned considered English Canadians to be somewhat hostile towards them. The APEC attack and rejection of the distinct society had been heavy blows, so much so that in an Angus Reid poll dated 11 June 1990, following ratification of Meech II, only 18 percent of Québécois considered that the Meech accord was a good one.[23]

SCARE STORIES

As it turns out, the prima donna-ish crises Bourassa regularly offered up to English Canada served no purpose. Without

Meech, he said, the world would stop turning and the sovereignists would come back to power in Quebec. How many times did we see him crying on English Canada's shoulder because he was the only head of government in the country who had a separatist opposition? Staking everything, Mulroney then adopted the same line. Canada would break up and economic crisis, including the collapse of the dollar and rising interest rates, would inevitably follow the failure of Meech.

The strategy didn't work, if only because it was solely a reaction to English Canada's increasingly pronounced rejection, and because it vastly under-estimated the profound opposition that existed in the rest of the country. The momentum now was definitely anti-Meech. And if Filmon seemed to give in to pressure on the night of 9 June 1990, he quickly took cover behind Elijah Harper in order to hold onto the support of his electorate and assign responsibility for rejecting the accord to the native people – while continuing to pass himself off as a victim of Mulroney.

While his threats of an as-yet-undefined superstructure or some mysterious alternative solution were being prepared, Bourassa was trying above all to break English-Canada's resistance. Relying on reports confirming the economic viability of a sovereign Quebec, he helped to create the absolutely bizarre impression that only English Canada would suffer economically from the eventual separation of Quebec. He promised the apocalypse to the West, the lost paradise to Quebec, and the bubonic plague to Newfoundland. If these curses managed to shake Wells's certainty, they still didn't cause English-Canadian public opinion to budge.

Bourassa's radical change of tone in the face of the intransigence of Wells, Filmon, and McKenna also set a new dynamic in motion in Canada. By playing the card of separatism, Bourassa greatly underestimated the extent of English Canada's opposition and fed Quebec's feelings of rejection even more. But the moment of truth had arrived. It came when Bourassa stated a truth which few wanted to hear, namely that English Canada probably needed Quebec more than the reverse. By saying this, Bourassa was locking himself inside a contradiction that undermined his credibility: if federalism was no longer really paying off for Quebec, why persist in wanting to rejoin the Canadian family?

THE CHAREST REPORT

Mulroney's supreme and ultimate blunder was the decision to accept McKenna's recommendations as a basis for the Charest Committee, while knowing full well that they would provoke Quebec's wrath and create expectations in English Canada that would be impossible to satisfy. It forced the increasingly cornered Quebec Liberals to vote for an even more "radical" version of a Parti Québécois motion refusing any possible change or amendment to the accord.

By shamelessly adding a shopping list to an accord that was already strongly watered down, the Charest Committee report, tabled in mid-May 1990, completely ignored the fact that Meech was supposed to reply exclusively to demands by Quebec. Jean Charest's willingness to be associated with such a process stems from a political opportunism that is liable to haunt him for a long time. Be that as it may, the report did at least serve to clarify once and for all what was at stake in the debate. It was becoming increasingly clear that the two solitudes were now on the point of colliding. It was then that the blood-letting among the Conservatives began, with the predictable departures of François Gérin and Lucien Bouchard. Since then, Mulroney has been severely criticized for bringing about his own misfortunes by inviting Quebec nationalists to run under the Conservative banner, and there are those who called Bouchard an opportunist, a fanatic, or a demagogue after his resignation.[24] But Bouchard had no choice. He had always promised that the accord would be adopted without modifications, and he was convinced that this was also the position of "his" government. However, several of the Charest Report's recommendations, even if they could have formed the basis of a parallel accord, contradicted the spirit and the letter of Meech Lake. Bouchard had reason, then, to feel betrayed.

The violent reaction against Bouchard in English Canada can be explained in part by a refusal to accept that, since the referendum, the situation in Quebec had become very complicated. In this sense, the presence of Bouchard and Gérin had forced English Canada to recognize the new reality of Quebec. On the other hand, their resignation had sounded the death knell for the renewed federalism whose authorship Trudeau now had the gall to deny! Unfortunately, however, people preferred to see in this a plot that was made possible by Mulroney's incompetence and his deliberate blindness. Whence the tremendous relief at seeing these "traitors" finally leave the Conservative party, and the hope that the new Bloc Québécois would fall apart as quickly as possible.[25]

HENCEFORTH, CANADA WILL BE A REAL COUNTRY...

When the premier of Quebec decided to go to the last ditch meeting in Ottawa, despite the advice of several Québécois nationalists, he entered into a dynamic from which he could not emerge a winner. To make the accord more acceptable to English Canada and allow the recalcitrant provinces to ratify it, he would have to make concessions. Even if these were skilfully masked and hidden behind the shattering mid-week departure of Bouchard and Gérin, they would be major. Claiming that Quebec would henceforth refuse to participate in any discussion about the distinct society (which would be refuted a few days later)[26], he nonetheless agreed to considerably weakening its impact.

The Ottawa marathon was above all a media spectacle. There were patriotic professions of faith by Joe Ghiz, Don Getty, and Peterson, as well as the turnaround by McKenna, who tried to make others forget his "miscalculation" about the consequences of rejecting Meech Lake. As for Bourassa, in the early hours of 10 June he proclaimed that "henceforth, with ratification of the accord, for all Quebeckers Canada will be a real country." Nevertheless, the "arm-twisting" sessions in Ottawa came within a hair's breadth of succeeding. Aided by apocalyptic scenarios and the Chrétien commando group, the support of the Manitoba trio was won, and even Wells began to have doubts.

HENCEFORTH, QUEBEC WILL BE A REAL COUNTRY...

Having absolutely no idea about what was going to happen in Manitoba, Bourassa was too quick to claim victory on his return from Ottawa, declaring that "the nationalist fever was only a flash in the pan."[27] Nothing, however, was going to stop the Meech Lake Accord from giving up the ghost on the date forecast. The "murderers" were numerous and, as could have been predicted, all were equally eager to deny that they had done it.

At first glance, one could always blame Elijah Harper for the failure. History will judge ironically the fact that, overnight, English Canada had discovered a passionate concern for a nation it had always treated as a sub-proletariat. Those who have travelled to the big cities in English Canada have seen this with their own eyes. What actually went on was the shameful use of one nation to fight another. After making the mistake of signing an accord that no one in Manitoba wanted, the Filmon-Doer-Carstairs trio managed to save face before a public that was clearly anti-Meech, while Wells, the wily scapegoat, could with full peace of mind renege on his promise to hold a vote in the Newfoundland House of Assembly. By so doing he avoided what he'd been afraid of from the outset: being the only one to refuse the accord.

It was then that, landing on his feet once more, Bourassa, the born-again Canadian, would give way to Bourassa the Head of State and Defender of Quebec's higher interests: "English Canada must understand very clearly that whatever is said and whatever is done, Quebec is now and forever a distinct society, free and able to assume its destiny."[28]

What a pity he didn't have that attitude one fine day in spring when he placed his signature on a document confirming that Quebec was prepared to get back in line for a mess of pottage ...

The Failure of the Accord:

Immediate Causes and Excuses

Ultimately, as the next chapter will attempt to show, the failure of the accord stems above all from the radically different and largely irreconcilable ways in which English Canada and Quebec perceive the Canadian reality. Nonetheless, there were various individuals and groups who contributed directly or indirectly to blocking the adoption of Meech Lake, notably the Trudeau/Chrétien duo, the recalcitrant provinces and their political leaders, native people, the anglophone minority in Quebec, and francophones outside Quebec. Similarly, events such as adoption of Bill 178, the NDP and Conservative leadership races, the 1988 victory of Brian Mulroney and free trade, and the process for adopting the accord, all helped undermine the Meech Lake Accord. In certain cases, events and groups played an important role; in others, they served basically as excuses, allowing the main actors to hide objectives and prejudices, unmentioned because unmentionable.

OPPOSITION BY GROUPS

At one level, we can identify a certain number of groups who were convinced that their preoccupations and priorities were being either threatened or ignored by the accord. Together, they represented an impressive political strike force. There was concern in particular that certain provisions of the accord would allow the government of Quebec to overstep some prescriptions of the charter.

Women's groups across Canada, for example, including the Canadian Council on the Status of Women, maintained that Article 16 of the accord authorized Quebec to promote its distinct nature at the expense of their rights. They demanded that the charter take full precedence over the entire Meech Lake Accord.[1] In Quebec, however, groups defending women's rights did not believe that the distinct nature of Quebec was a threat to the principle of equality of the sexes. Some Quebec commentators expressed doubts as to the sincerity of these allegations. As Lysiane Gagnon observed: "What is at the bottom of this unsolicited concern? Could it by any chance be a roundabout and in fact nicely hypocritical way of attacking the distinct society clause simply because they oppose such recognition, because they want a homogeneous country but don't dare to come right out and say so?"[2]

As far as the ethnic groups were concerned, they denounced the fact that the fundamental characteristics of the country should be defined in linguistic terms and asked that the accord recognize Canada's multicultural nature. According to these groups, the Meech Lake Accord subordinated multiculturalism to linguistic duality and to Quebec's distinct nature. There were fears that Quebec would hold back multiculturalism inside the province, to the benefit of the French language and culture.[3]

Opposition by native people, which was pushed to the foreground by the spectacular behaviour of NDP member Elijah Harper during the dying days of Meech, had nevertheless been present since the early days of the saga. Fuelled by native bitterness in the face of Canada's refusal to recognize their constitutional rights, this opposition was reinforced by the situation in the spring of 1987. That March, in fact, constitutional negotiations on native rights had once again failed miserably.[4]

From the outset, natives were convinced that adopting the Meech Lake Accord would postpone indefinitely one of their most cherished claims, the right to self-government. And in their opinion the accord was seriously flawed because the new interpretation of the constitution (linguistic duality – distinct society) did not recognize their presence as a fundamental characteristic of Canada, and because only Quebec would have acquired the status of a distinct society. According to native chiefs, this was an implicit admission that there were no other distinct societies in Canada, otherwise they would have been specifically identified. They saw nothing in the accord that, from a constitutional point of view, would enable them to advance their rights.

Like some other Canadians, notably those in the "disadvantaged" provinces, native peoples who benefitted from federal socio-economic programs feared the possible effects on these programs of what they saw as the decentralizing nature of the accord. Finally, natives who had long been demanding the creation of provinces in the Yukon and Northwest Territories, where they formed a majority, worried about the effect of broadening the unanimity rule on the creation of new provinces.

For obvious political reasons, the Quebec anglophone community did not oppose distinct society status for Quebec, so long as this recognition was symbolic and, above all, would not expand Quebec's powers to promote the French language. Alliance-Quebec advocated the explicit precedence of the charter over the distinct society clause, abolition of the notwithstanding clause, elimination of Quebec's power to participate in naming three judges to the Supreme Court, as well as recognition of federal and provincial government responsibility for promoting linguistic duality, i.e., bilingualism. In a word, they wanted a complete re-negotiation of the accord.[5]

Satisfied with the charter judgments handed down on Bill 101, the anglophone minority may have been afraid of seeing the charter's effectiveness diminished in favour of the distinct society.[6] But it is difficult to understand the anglo-Quebec community's opposition to an accord that explicitly recognized it, and whose rights and privileges were given ample protection by the duality rule. It would appear then that the very notion of a distinct society put off some of them to the point where they were unable to support any accord that contained such a provision.

The anglophones' most devastating impact on the Meech Lake Accord, however, unquestionably came from their opposition to Bill 178 and the image of Quebec which they conveyed to English Canada. By casting themselves as martyrs, spokespersons for the community simply fuelled English-Canadian prejudices, while salving their own consciences regarding their treatment of francophone minorities. Not to mention references to the notwithstanding clause as showing the hideous face the distinct society could assume ...

William Johnson's hysterical columns in *The Gazette* helped to discredit Quebec and the Québécois and fanned English-Canadian opposition to the accord by presenting a distorted image of the Quebec reality. Alliance-Quebec even went to New Brunswick and asked Frank McKenna to continue blocking the accord.

It was all very effective: a poll conducted in February 1990 showed that a majority of English Canadians believed their francophone minorities were better treated than were anglo-Quebeckers. The disproportionate and irresponsible reactions to Bill 178 by certain leaders of the anglophone community fuelled not only anti-Meech sentiments but anti-francophone feelings as well. Thus, shortly after adoption of Bill 178, the governments of Saskatchewan and Alberta repealed the linguistic provisions of the law governing the Northwest Territories, replacing them with far more restricted guarantees; the Manitoba Court of Appeal ruled that francophones did not have the right to administer their own schools; and Saskatchewan passed Bill 2 pertaining to the use of French and English in the province which, according to the Official Languages Commissioner, constituted "clearly a step backwards." According to

Guy Matte, president of the Fédération des francophones hors Québec, "The situation of French-Canadians living outside Quebec would improve dramatically if English-speaking Quebeckers told the rest of the country they are not a persecuted minority."[7]

Nevertheless, it was francophones outside Quebec who launched the first serious attacks on the accord. Fearing that a distinct Quebec would be increasingly French, and that the rest of Canada would become increasingly English, the francophone minorities tried to encourage the federal government to obtain a mandate not only to preserve linguistic duality but to promote it. New Brunswick Acadians wanted, in addition to recognition of the equality of the province's two linguistic communities as a fundamental characteristic of New Brunswick, the governments of both Canada and New Brunswick to be assigned the role of protecting and promoting these communities.[8] According to Yvon Fontaine, dean of law at l'Université de Moncton:

With a protective role only, it is highly probable that there is no obligation to legislate to the advantage of the two communities. The role of protecting ... would impose at most the duty of non-discrimination or non-assimilation. For that reason it would be desirable if Parliament were given the role to protect and promote Canadian duality, rather than merely protect it.[9]

Adding insult to injury, the combined effect of the safeguard clause and the English provinces' obligation to protect but not promote duality actually removed from francophones outside Quebec any chance of expanding their rights – while Quebec was obliged to promote its distinct character, of which the anglophone minority was explicitly a part. Like the 1867 constitution, Meech thereby granted preferential treatment to English Quebeckers.

We tend to forget that at Mont Gabriel in May 1986 the government of Quebec had presented a sixth condition aimed at improving the situation of francophones outside Quebec. This proposal was rejected because of opposition by some of the western premiers. The francophones outside Quebec weren't mistaken, then, when they accused Robert Bourassa of abandoning them.

Leaders of the francophone minorities hesitated between lukewarm approval of Meech and outright opposition to it. Such reluctance served Premier McKenna and his counterpart Gary Filmon wonderfully well, as they were then able to evoke a "noble cause" to explain part of their opposition. Following pressure from Quebec and the federal government, and with a growing conviction that they were liable to be the big losers should Meech fail, the francophones outside Quebec finally rallied behind the accord. It was not until February 1990, a few months before the deadline, that the FFHQ (Fédération des francophones hors Québec) and the Société nationale des Acadiens reversed their stand and came out in favour of Meech Lake.

Demands by groups opposed to the accord, though often legitimate, mainly served the interests of the recalcitrant provinces and of those seeking an excuse for refusing to recognize the distinct society.

THE TRUDEAU/CHRÉTIEN DUO: TO ENGLISH CANADA'S RESCUE

In ideological and partisan terms, intervention by the Trudeau/Chrétien duo was decisive in the failure of Meech Lake. The first crushing blow was dealt by Pierre Trudeau after the first ministers' agreement in principle on 30 April 1987. In a virulent outburst, the former prime minister claimed that the accord had rendered Canada impotent, that it conceded too many powers to the provinces, and that it represented an unacceptable capitulation to Quebec nationalists by offering them more than they themselves had asked for. He accused Prime

Minister Mulroney of being weak and cowardly – a wimp. He was especially hard on the distinct society which, he claimed, destroyed the dream of a united, bilingual and multicultural Canada, and he condemned the federal government for surrendering its absolute powers to appoint senators and Supreme Court judges.

Robert Bourassa, one of the former prime minister's favorite whipping boys, came in for some slaps as well. Trudeau accused him of using blackmail, Quebec's favorite tool for achieving its goals, and of leading the other provinces down the same road. He blamed him for not feeling bound by the Canada Act of 1982 and for choosing to continue the Péquiste struggle, thereby accepting the nationalist claims that, throughout Canada's constitutional evolution, Quebec had constantly been had.

Trudeau's outburst had a considerable impact on English Canada, and by shattering the unanimity of Quebec it set off and legitimized some violent reactions against the accord. It enabled the propagation of the tenacious myth that Quebec was pulling the wool over English Canada's eyes. It actually came within a hair's breadth of wrecking the 2 June meeting at Ottawa's Langevin Building. On that occasion the first ministers negotiated for nineteen consecutive hours before reaching final agreement on the legal formulation of the Meech Accord. According to someone close to Bourassa:

You can't imagine how hard Peterson was on that day, 2 June ... On 20 April the Ontario leader had been one of those to speak most favorably about the return of Quebec to the Canadian "family." On 2 June he came back to concessions made a month before. Trudeau's stunning intervention in the debate caused a stir in Ontario public opinion and the Liberal leader couldn't ignore it.

Over the next three years, Trudeau made a few more conspicuous political interventions. On 30 March 1988, testifying before the Senate Committee on the accord, he again attacked Mulroney, accusing him of having conceded tremendous powers to the provinces in exchange for temporary peace in federal-provincial relations. He recommended that the Senate block the accord by amending it, which it did on 21 April 1988. Nine amendments were proposed, notably the explicit subordination of the "distinct society" clause to the Charter of Rights. On 22 June, then, the House of Commons was once more obliged to ratify the accord in order to overrule the Senate's proposed amendments. Slowly but surely, doubt settled in and the opponents' position was reinforced.

Trudeau's campaign against Meech Lake was also the occasion for the launching of two books. *With a Bang, Not a Whimper: Pierre Trudeau Speaks Out* reprinted some of the former prime minister's earlier articles, but the attack on the accord continued, especially in the final chapter. In 1990, a few months before the Meech deadline, he co-edited, with Thomas Axworthy, *Towards A Just Society: The Trudeau Years*,[10] in which, with the help of a dozen of the faithful from the old days, notably Gérard Pelletier, Marc Lalonde, Jacques Hébert, Lloyd Axworthy, and John Roberts, he offered a self-satisfied and grossly partisan assessment of his reign. Jean Chrétien's contribution on repatriating the Constitution is a pitiful justification of one of the most sordid episodes in Canadian political history. Denying that he wanted to get involved in the Meech debate, Trudeau nevertheless undertook a cross-Canada tour during which he talked mostly about ... Meech. As if it could have been otherwise under the circumstances.

The former prime minister also got involved in the Liberal leadership race. After trying to convince Marc Lalonde, "his most brilliant heir apparent," he finally fell back on Chrétien. Trudeau told Chrétien that his criticisms of Meech Lake were too moderate, and warned the leadership hopeful that his support was not unconditional.[11] Throughout the debate, Trudeau never missed a chance to reassure English Canada, saying that the threat of independence should the accord be rejected was only a "hoax."[12]

After the failed attempt to abort Meech Lake at the federal level, it became obvious that the battle was going to be waged in the provincial legislatures. Trudeau lavished advice on Manitoba's Sharon Carstairs, New Brunswick's McKenna, and above all, on Newfoundland's Clyde Wells. Multiplying phone calls, informal advice, and consultations through third parties, he provided the arguments and ideas with which they could express their opposition to Meech. More often than not, Wells's speeches read like out-and-out copies of Trudeau's declarations. Similarly, before he delivered his first major speech on the question during the leadership race, Chrétien sought his former boss's imprimatur. In Calgary, on 22 June 1990, Trudeau savored his triumph through frenzied accolades with Wells and Chrétien. During a brief address to native people, he let out a vibrant "I love you," thanking the chiefs of the first nations for having saved Canada by sinking Meech.

If Trudeau was the ideological detonator in the failure of Meech, Chrétien was the accord's true destroyer. Following the first ministers' meeting in April 1987, however, he had said he was "very happy" for his friend Bourassa. The collapse of Meech Lake was brought about by the shattering of the consensus in the Liberal Party of Canada and among Quebec federalists. Even if the Liberals supported the accord, opposition by the "Chrétien wing" guaranteed that several elements in the party would defect. According to most Manitoba observers, it was the relentless determination of Liberal leader Carstairs, a Chrétien disciple who had had his active support during the 1988 provincial election, that dealt the death blow to the accord in that province. Similarly, by breaking the unity of federalist Quebec, the Trudeau/Chrétien duo legitimized the turnaround of a good part of English Canada on a promise made in June 1987. It is unlikely, even unthinkable, that Wells or

57

McKenna, two Liberal premiers, would have rejected the accord had unanimity prevailed within both the federal Liberals and federalist Quebec.

Chrétien's leadership campaign provided an opportunity not only to capitalize on English Canada's opposition to Meech by pocketing delegates but also to both support it and stir it up. Like Trudeau, Chrétien did all he could to be reassuring about the consequences of rejecting the accord and to give credence to the notion that Quebec was bluffing. Among the insipid metaphors he served up, the best was undoubtedly the one in which he compared Canadian constitutional problems to a car stuck in a snowbank; all that was needed to get out of the rut was to go forward a little, then back up a little ... And "if we don't settle it on 23 June, we'll settle it next year."[13] According to Ralph Surette, a Nova Scotia Acadian journalist, the Atlantic provinces' opposition to the accord and Wells's sangfroid may be explained because there was remarkable confidence in Liberal circles that Chrétien could deliver what he had promised: to re-establish the federal presence in Quebec and prevent the Québécois from packing up and leaving.[14] According to Lysiane Gagnon, Trudeau's disciple provided opponents of Meech with a forceful argument: "In his pea-soup accent, he swore by all that's holy that Quebeckers wouldn't budge if Meech should sink, and that should Quebec react with some vague sovereignist stirrings, he would bring them to their senses. The proof: he was the one who had picked up the majority of Quebec delegates."[15]

At a number of levels, then, the leadership race would be only a tasteless "remake" of Trudeau's rise in the late 1960s. In English Canada, Chrétien presented himself as a kind of insurance policy against any attempt by the Quebec people to increase their bargaining power even slightly, even within the federal framework. In Quebec, he was much more subtle, never failing to point out that he had always supported Quebec's five conditions.

In the final months, and particularly the final weeks, before the ultimate deadline, assured of the support of a strong majority of delegates to the leadership convention, and having measured the gravity of the situation, Chrétien set out to revise his strategy. It had become apparent even to him that the failure of Meech would have unpleasant consequences for supporters of national unity, and that, contrary to his earlier claims, it would be impossible simply to start from scratch. Panicking, he already saw himself negotiating the sovereignty of Quebec on behalf of English Canada, or perhaps quite simply trying to persuade the anglophone provinces that he could represent them in such negotiations. In a word, the prospect of a very big snowbank.

Even though he had always said that the accord would be rejected and that a parallel accord couldn't meet his objections, Chrétien worked actively and directly on the contents of the Charest report, whose recommendations he and the Liberal delegation endorsed. Later, he appeared ready to accept – not publicly, of course – that no amendment would explicitly make the "distinct society" subordinate to the Charter of Rights. During the final marathon in Ottawa, while cloaking himself in total silence and literally disappearing from public view, he worked relentlessly along with his advisors, who were surprised more than once working the corridors at the conference, bringing Carstairs and Wells into line. His efforts came very close to being rewarded. For the Québécois people, Chrétien's opposition to Meech, his pseudo-turnarounds, and his opportunism were seen at best as contempuous, at worst as a betrayal. In English Canada, where "the little guy from Shawinigan" had previously been regarded as a saviour, doubt was settling in. Even the magazine *Saturday Night*, which regularly parades its nostalgia for Trudeau, asked some hard questions in its June 1990 issue about the substance of a man who, without his advisors and when left to his own devices, was generally poorly informed and uninspiring.

By one of those strokes of irony to which history alone holds
the secret, the Trudeau/Chrétien duo, by torpedoing the
Meech constitutional project, has contributed to accelerating
the disintegration of Canada.

THE RECALCITRANT PROVINCES

If anyone had wanted deliberately to bring about the failure of
the accord, they could have done no better than to suggest a
three-year ratification process. Over that long period, there was
a shift in Canadian public opinion from indifference to outright
hostility. After the stinging defeat in Quebec of both the Liberals and the NDP in the 1988 federal election, and with accu-
sations of treason being levelled at Quebec for having
supported free trade, the fine unanimity of the federal parties
in favour of Meech Lake was shattered. Electoral opportunism
quickly gave way to the true convictions of both Liberals and
NDP. At its leadership convention in December 1989, the NDP
confirmed its turnaround by electing Audrey McLaughlin, a
steadfast opponent of Meech. For the Liberals, support for the
accord did not end officially until 23 June 1990, with the
election of Chrétien to replace John Turner, who had been a
faithful supporter to the very end. That endless death-watch
also saw three provincial elections and the rejection of the
accord by the three new governments.

McKenna, who was elected on 13 October 1987 on an anti-
Meech platform, led off. He has the dubious honour of having
established the precedent whereby a newly elected first minister can renege on the word and the signature of his predecessor. McKenna insisted on major amendments to Meech,
including the assurance that federal aid to the disadvantaged
provinces wouldn't be touched, constitutional recognition of
New Brunswick's bilingualism, a role in promoting Canadian
duality for the federal government, and certain constitutional
guarantees for women and native people.

Some months before the deadline, the New Brunswick premier realized that, contrary to the certainties expressed by the Trudeau/Chrétien duo, there was a danger that the failure of Meech would lead to the break-up of Canada; now his own demands struck him as secondary. He noted too that the Pandora's box he had opened had brought numerous anti-francophone and anti-Quebec extremists to public attention. McKenna then decided to take an active part in a rescue operation to be controlled from a distance by the federal government. He agreed to table in the New Brunswick legislature an accompanying resolution that was to explore the foundations of a possible compromise. This resolution, or rather the proposed process, was quickly ratified by Mulroney and served as a backdrop for the Charest Report. Finally, McKenna was the first to leave the clan of the dissident provinces when, shortly before the deadline, he had his legislature adopt the accord, even though he had not obtained most of the amendments he was after.

Globe and Mail columnist Jeffrey Simpson summed up the New Brunswick premier's tragic personal saga:

Mr McKenna made a ghastly mistake, and he knows it. The getting of wisdom came to him late, far too late, but when it came he could see the outline of the national disingegration he had contributed to setting in motion, and it made him sad ... At some point in the Meech Lake debate, Mr. McKenna began to get scared. He could see the demons of disunity running loose across the country, doing their nasty work, setting up a far more difficult situation for Canada, and for linguistically divided New Brunswick, than anything contemplated in Meech Lake ... It's a mistake that will torment Mr. McKenna, a generous and now much wiser man, for the rest of his political life.[16]

On 26 April 1988, Conservative Gary Filmon was elected as head of a minority government in Manitoba. The NDP, whose leader Howard Pawley had supported the Accord when he was premier and who had resigned before the election, wound up in third place behind Carstairs' Liberals. The new NDP leader, Gary Doer, and Carstairs, encouraged by Manitoba public opinion which was running strongly against the accord, and spurred by the growing opposition of federal Conservatives and NDP, rejected Meech categorically. From his minority position, Premier Filmon sought some excuse for not tabling the accord in the Manitoba legislature.

His chance came when the Quebec government decided to exclude itself from the Supreme Court judgment on the language of signs by invoking the notwithstanding clause. The next day, 19 December 1988, a resolution in support of Meech was withdrawn from the Manitoba legislative agenda. Filmon condemned Bill 178 as being contrary to "the spirit of Meech Lake." Since Manitoba was the province that had most consistently and most effectively opposed the rights of its francophone minority, Filmon's sudden outburst in support of the oppressed anglophone minority of Quebec seems odd. To keep up appearances, one might have hoped for a more credible excuse. Even the *Winnipeg Free Press* declared in an editorial that Bill 178 was merely an excuse, and that the real reason for withdrawing from the accord was the growing opposition of the Manitoba population.[17] The writer also suggested that Filmon would have trouble convincing francophones that he was a fervent defender of minority linguistic rights when he had fought against broadening those rights in Manitoba in 1983–84.

Similarly, in Canada overall the adoption of Bill 178 allowed some opponents of Meech to disguise and conceal their rejection of Quebec by pleading the noble cause of individual rights. The argument could have aroused a certain sympathy if it had not, in most cases, been the prerogative of the most anti-Québécois and anti-francophone elements in Canadian society. Moreover, as Gordon Robertson, the former Clerk of the Privy Council declared, "Bill 178 ... [is] not a fair gauge of the state of the rights of anglophones in Quebec. Those rights are considerably more extensive today than the rights of the French-speaking minority in any province."[18] He added that the events in Sault-Ste-Marie and Thunder Bay were probably linked with Bill 178 in some confused way, but that resentment in those cities stemmed principally from financial concerns and from anti-francophone prejudices.

In Manitoba, the 1986 federal government decision to award a CF-18 maintenance contract to Bombardier (Canadair), despite the recommendation of an Ottawa task force in favour of Winnipeg's Bristol Aerospace, also helped sustain bitterness towards Quebec and the federal government. Although the impact on Meech is hard to measure, it was probably considerable.

On 3 March 1989, Filmon announced the creation of a seven-member tripartite committee with a mandate to hold public hearings on the accord across the province. These took place between 6 April and 2 May, and more than 300 persons were heard. Three out of four were opposed to ratification. Numerous speakers displayed strong resentment of both central Canada and francophones. The task force recommendations tackled the very substance of the accord, and Quebec's five conditions were, to varying degrees, deemed unacceptable. There was no question of a parallel accord. The agreement would have to be re-opened and amendments and major modifications brought in. Proposals by the task force included: rejection of any restriction on federal spending powers; refusal of unanimity on constitutional changes affecting the senate and the creation of new provinces; and a "Canada clause" that would include as fundamental characteristics the existence of native peoples, multiculturalism, the role of the federal Parliament in "safeguarding" Canada's fundamental characteristics, "the existence of Canada as a federal state enjoying a distinct national identity," and the absolute primacy of the Canadian Charter of Rights and Freedoms over Quebec's distinct society.

The arm-twisting operation by Mulroney and the federal machine, the growing economic crisis, fears about national unity, and belated pressure by Chrétien would finally break the resistance of the three Manitoba parties and, with a notorious lack of will and enthusiasm, they undertook to ratify the accord. Many would greet Elijah Harper's manoeuvres as a blessing, one that gave them the result they wanted on the backs of native people and, above all, didn't require them to assume any responsibility for it.

On 20 April 1989, Liberal Clyde Wells came to power in Newfoundland. Just hours after his election, he too erupted against the accord. In particular, he claimed that it would give Quebec special status, make senate reform almost impossible, and weaken the powers of the federal government.

Wells, like Trudeau, had grossly overestimated the decentralizing nature of the accord. As premier of a disadvantaged province, it was normal that he should be concerned about the federal government's ability to continue making transfer payments. However, through his role in the rejection, the Newfoundland premier, like Filmon and McKenna, who also represented poorer provinces, opened the door to a re-examination of Canadian federation that went far deeper than did Meech Lake. His province would in fact be one of the big losers should Quebec become sovereign.

Wells also channelled and stirred up anti-francophone, anti-bilingual, and anti-Québécois feelings across the country. This was stunningly confirmed by a *Globe and Mail* – CBC poll published on 9 July 1990. According to George Perlin, a Queen's political scientist and advisor to the Canadian Facts polling firm: "Some of the support for Premier Wells comes from those people who shared his critique of the principles in the Meech Lake accord, but much of his support comes from people who took what might be considered anti-French positions."[19]

More than other Canadians, then, Wells's followers had little sympathy for the aspirations of Quebec, were opposed to any form of protection for the French language inside or outside Quebec, and approved of the attitudes toward English unilingualism of people in cities like Sault-Ste-Marie and Thunder

Bay. Throughout the debate, the Newfoundland premier showed a notorious lack of understanding toward Quebec. His acts of faith in favour of pan-Canadian bilingualism don't stand up to analysis. The situation of Newfoundland's francophone minority is actually disastrous, and it took a court decision before the first French school was opened in St John's in 1989.

If Wells had the "courage" to follow the Meech saga to the end, it was because he knew he was supported by the majority of Canadians and backed by the "French Canadians" Trudeau and Chrétien. After the defeat of Meech, he was seen across Canada (except in Quebec) as the most popular politician in the country and the one who had given the best performance during the debate. His ratings were ten times higher than Mulroney's, and far higher than Peterson's.[20] As will be seen in the next chapter, Wells's themes faithfully reflect the concerns of English Canada; they also agree with those of Trudeau, particularly with respect to maintaining a centralizing federal government and a strong national identity.

To bring about the failure of Meech, Trudeau and Chrétien became the allies of the most reactionary and most anti-francophone forces in the country. History will judge them severely. Accordingly, the triumphant embraces of Wells, Trudeau and Chrétien were profoundly indecent and should remain fixed forever in the collective memory of the Québécois.

The final closed retreat in Ottawa, where he was bulldozed by the federal government and abandoned by Manitoba, almost spelled the end of the indomitable Wells. Isolated, shaken, but still convinced that rejection of the accord would not have the anticipated impact on the economy or national unity, he nonetheless agreed, most reluctantly, to put his opposition on hold and submit Meech to his legislature. Once he was back home, though, the Harper episode in Manitoba gave him an unhoped-for pretext to avoid holding a vote in the Newfoundland House of Assembly. In all likelihood, however, that vote would have confirmed rejection of Meech. By deciding not to hold it, Wells

was simply trying to reduce the weight of the historical responsibility that Newfoundland would have to bear.

SOME OTHER EXCUSES ...

There are those who will try to blame the flaws in Mulroney's
strategy for the ultimate failure of the accord. Even though
there is no doubt that errors in judgment occurred, particularly
in holding the first ministers' meeting in Ottawa too late and
Mulroney's boast about his "throw of the dice," it's hard to
imagine any strategy that would have allowed such an operation
to succeed despite massive opposition from English Canada. In
fact, by managing to persuade Quebec to be satisfied with so
little in order to "rejoin" the Constitution, convincing all the
provinces to accept the accord at the outset, and, finally, "forc-
ing" a final consensus (leaving aside the conditional signature
of Wells) in the early days at Ottawa, the case could even be
made that Mulroney had played his hand very well.

From the standpoint of national unity and the failure of
Meech, the grossest errors were committed by those who realized the consequences of rejection too late. These include the
chief spokespersons for linguistic minorities, New Brunswick
Premier McKenna, who was a detonator of provincial opposition, and Chrétien, whose salvage operation was too late and
too qualified.

Criticisms about the anti-democratic nature of the procedure
were just another excuse, even though I myself am convinced
that any significant constitutional change should be submitted
to the population through a referendum. The June 1987
accord had been discussed for a year before being adopted by
the first ministers. It was then submitted to all the legislatures
for adoption over a period of three years. There was nothing
to prevent public hearings and parliamentary commissions in
all the provinces. Technically, the accord failed as a result of
opposition by a single MNA, and according to the way a single

legislature chose to interpret its rules. This no doubt speaks volumes about the relatively democratic nature of the undertaking ...

By comparison, the amending process Trudeau initiated in 1981 was much more authoritarian. Major changes to the Constitution were made without public consultation, with no general election or referendum, and despite strong opposition by both parties in Quebec's National Assembly. The profound hypocrisy of those who were scandalized by the process has to do with the fact that it was those same individuals who applauded the 1981–82 operation.

A New English Canada?

Beyond the individuals, groups, and parties who contributed to the failure of Meech, and beyond the excuses used to justify their opposition, the accord's foundering can be explained basically by the emergence in English Canada of a vision of the country which is largely incompatible and irreconcilable with the one Quebec has advocated for several decades. Even if Meech had passed, it would have been only a matter of time before relations between Quebec and Canada were called into question.

It is necessary to remember that, contrary to what we are often encouraged to believe, opposition to Meech was never limited to a few politicians or marginal provinces. Poll after poll has shown that opposition in English Canada went much deeper. An Angus Reid poll conducted early in April 1990 showed that 59 percent of the Canadian population was opposed to Meech Lake, and only 24 percent in favour.[1] If Quebec, the only province where the accord had more supporters than opponents, is excluded, rejection was that much clearer. In other regions of the country, a strong proportion of respondents said that they disapproved of the accord: 74 percent in Saskatchewan and Manitoba, 73 percent in British Columbia, 66 percent in Ontario, 65 percent in the Maritimes, and 64 percent in Alberta.

Opposition was expressed both to the *spirit* of the accord and to its specific contents. A March 1990 Gallup poll, for example, demonstrated that 53 percent of Canadians were opposed to Quebec's being considered a "distinct society," as opposed to only 27 percent in favour of that notion.[2] In addition, a CBC–*Globe and Mail* poll confirmed that 82 percent of the Canadian population (excluding Quebec) was opposed to Quebec's exercising the right to pass laws affecting French language and culture (including laws that might come into conflict with the Canadian Charter of Rights and Freedoms).[3] This was a clear denial of any claim to primacy which Quebec might maintain in this field.

Beyond the insidious work of the Trudeau/Chrétien duo, why was there such massive disapproval in English Canada? At one level, there is obviously strong anti-Quebec and anti-francophone sentiment. Debates on the accord encouraged the spectacular coming out of the closet by whatever remained of the old Orangists who believed that bilingualism posed a threat to the English language and would inevitably led to French unilingualism across the country. Here too, Bill 178 served as a pretext for individuals and provinces who had been fighting the French fact for decades.

Even if a good part of the Canadian elite continued to advocate pan-Canadian bilingualism as the only acceptable solution to the Quebec "problem," support for bilingualism across the country is eroding. In July 1990, a slim majority of 50 percent of Canadians disapproved of resolutions declaring Sault-Ste-Marie and Thunder Bay to be unilingually English.[4] Generally, people declared themselves not in favour of any extensions of bilingual policies. According to Queen's University political scientist George Perlin, "People accept the principle of bilingualism, but as soon as concrete policies have to be adopted, they rebel."[5] In Canada, moreover, there were more and more reservations about the Official Languages Act. That was why, according to Official Languages Commissioner D'Iberville Fortier, the federal government had not yet been bold enough to table regulations that would give a meaning to Bill C-72, passed more than two years earlier. Partly because of this absence of regulations, the new provisions of the act have had no impact in at least 80 percent of federal institutions.[6]

But, unquestionably, it is in the provinces and cities of English Canada that opposition to institutional bilingualism has been fiercest. In Manitoba, for example, the 1979 Supreme Court decision confirming the bilingualism of the provincial legislature was accepted very unwillingly. Similarly, in 1988 Saskatchewan and Alberta reacted negatively to the imposition of bilingualism. In February 1990, the town council of Sault-Ste-Marie, Ontario, claiming it wanted to "celebrate multiculturalism" by refusing to grant preferential treatment to the francophone minority, adopted a resolution making English the town's only official language.[7]

In fact, few Canadians identified with Pierre Trudeau's linguistic utopia. The race towards bilingualism in federal institutions was largely artificial and intended mainly to contain the fervor of Quebec nationalism. Too often, we tend to forget that Trudeau won election in English Canada only once, in 1968. In other elections he always had a minority. Moreover, "Trudeau distorted the message of the Royal Commission on Bilingualism and Biculturalism."[8] Although the commission clearly recognized the principle of the equality of the two dominant nations, Trudeau preferred to back the equality of official language minorities as well as bilingualism.

Finally, we should not forget that for some years Canada's socio-demographic composition has been evolving rapidly, greatly influencing political perceptions. Like it or not, bilingualism and the notion of two founding peoples no longer corresponds to the reality with which a large number of Canadians identify. Canada has become a multicultural country, and in a number of regions francophones occupy a smaller place than do other minorities. To English-Canadian eyes, then, francophones in Quebec or elsewhere are nothing more than just another ethnic group, in no way distinct and certainly not entitled to expect special treatment. In years to come this position, which is completely unacceptable to Quebec, will inevitably become more pronounced.

With Meech Lake, many anglophones had had their fill of constitutional questions and Quebec's demands. Hadn't Trudeau promised them that national reconciliation and the solution to the Quebec problem would come about through an idea of Canada based on federal primacy in the promotion of linguistic and cultural rights, including institutional bilingualism and a better fate for the francophone minorities? And it was thought at the time that the 1982 patriation would check Quebec's vague desires for autonomy once and for all by advancing the kind of renewed federalism that the vast majority of Québécois had been advocating for years. Through his desire to put down the "separatists" for good, Trudeau also duped English Canada, which ultimately found itself with an accord being offered to Quebec to compensate for the failure of the 1982 reform. Quebec having quite obviously become "insatiable," there was no reason to satisfy its aspirations, since in any case it would keep coming back for more ...

ENGLISH CANADA IN SEARCH OF ITS OWN DISTINCT SOCIETY

At a much more basic level, one of the great revelations of the Meech Lake debate, one that went largely unnoticed in Quebec where little is known or said about English Canada, was the evolution and the transformation of Canadian nationalism over the past few years. Over a long period, for tactical and opportunist reasons and in the name of pluralism and diversity, our anglophone compatriots denied the very existence of the entity that is English Canada. All the Québécois political players who were seeking to reconstruct the country on a bi-national basis inevitably encountered this argument.[9]

Moreover, the Québécois themselves have often denied the existence of the English-Canadian reality. Yet the debates surrounding Meech Lake and Free Trade clearly brought out a desire on the part of most English Canadians to maintain, in spite of obvious economic, geographic, linguistic, and cultural links with the rest of North America, a socio-political entity, distinct and different from the United States. Although shared values aren't always immediately obvious, although consensus is often minimal and heterogeneity undeniable, the will to survive, and also perhaps the fear of disappearing, are, in contrast, indisputable.

Beyond rejecting Quebec and its distinctness, the Meech Lake debate was very revealing about English Canada's priorities and political concerns. While unwilling to admit it, during those three long years English Canada was essentially defending the constitutional status quo. There was of course the desire that Quebec remain part of Canada, but while respecting already established structures and rules. Compared with this goal, the various demands of the recalcitrant provinces – senate reform, constitutional recognition of native rights, promotion of minorities, etc. – were clearly secondary.

Rejection of the distinct society, of any special status for Quebec or of any form of asymmetrical federation, can be explained in part by the desire to reinforce the Canadian identity and safeguard federal government powers. Among politicians, there is no doubt that Wells better than anyone else has articulated what could be called a "neo-Trudeauite" vision. For him, the Canadian Charter of Rights and Freedoms represents the instrument for developing a Canadian "nation,"[10] as well as an absolute rampart for protecting individual rights and freedoms: "The Canadian Charter is now the key component of our constitution that articulates the fundamental values which define us as Canadians and simply cannot be casually undermined."[11]

Wells was demanding, then, that individual rights take absolute precedence over collective rights, and consequently he advocated repeal of the notwithstanding clause. In Quebec, moreover, the emphasis has always been on the negative political consequences of the charter, including its centralizing aims as well as the limits it imposes on linguistic policy.[12]

Like most of the accord's opponents in English Canada, the Newfoundland premier did not object to having Quebec recognized as a distinct society in the preamble to the Constitution; rather, he rejected any implication or consequence in terms of rights or powers that could follow from this status. In the name of provincial equality, he refused any special legislative role for Quebec, which he maintained necessarily implied a superior status for the citizens of Quebec. And yet, as we have seen, Wells was getting worked up over nothing because the accord granted no new power to the provinces, nor did it in any way confer a special status that would have allowed Quebec to play "its role as the principal homeland of the French language and culture in Canada."[13]

This is because, for English Canadians as a whole, provincial identity is clearly secondary to Canadian identity. For Wells; "there is more to being a Canadian than being a resident of a particular province or territory. We have a sense of national citizenship and community that transcends our provincial identities ... Canada has a national identity that is more than the sum of its parts."[14]

Moreover, a January 1990 *Maclean's*/Decima poll showed that Quebeckers were the only Canadians (aside from Newfoundlanders, who had joined Confederation in 1949), who identified with their province first.[15] Quebec is the first place of national identification for the franco-Québécois. It is not surprising that numerous polls have shown that a large majority of Québécois support strong provincial governments, whereas English Canadians prefer to bank on the central government.[16] Many English Canadians, moreover, demonstrate a fair degree of contempt and suspicion towards provincial governments and their local or (far more pejoratively) parochial interests.[17]

For Wells and Canadian nationalists, another key element of the "Canadian national community" is the commitment to an equitable redistribution and sharing of resources among all Canadians, "furthering economic development to reduce disparity in opportunities, and providing essential public services of reasonable quality to all Canadians."[18] For Wells, then, no limits should be placed on the federal government's capacity to intervene, for it alone can attain such a goal, even if that implies regular and massive forays into fields under provincial jurisdiction. At this level, obviously, the impact of Meech Lake in English Canada was largely psychological. It's hard to see how the accord could have prevented the federal government from putting forward national social programs and led to decentralization and the "balkanization" of the country. Similarly, when English Canada opposes a role for the provinces in making nominations to the Supreme Court and the Senate because of a belief that doing so would contribute to a fragmentation of the Canadian identity, it denies the very essence of federalism.

Historically, federalism has been to a large extent imposed on English Canadians by a Quebec concerned about protecting its difference. Quebec is obviously perceived increasingly as a strait-jacket that is keeping Canada from realizing its legitimate aspirations. A majority of Canadians consider that Meech Lake would have weakened the Canadian identity. The vision that emerges is one of a desire for a highly centralized Canada. There is an implicit rejection of the possibility that reconciling multiple identities can be a factor for cohesion rather than division.

THE TRAUMA OF FREE TRADE

For English-Canadian nationalists, adoption of a free trade treaty with the United States was a traumatic experience. Rejection of Americanization was now on the agenda. More than ever, in order to face up to the challenge of marginalization, Canada looked to a strong central state to achieve a minimum of coherence and increase the scope of Canada's economy, culture, and society. According to political scientist Philip Resnick:

Without that control there really cannot be a Canadian (or English-Canadian) nation. Over the century and a quarter since Confederation, our symbols of nationhood have been associated with it. From mounted police to railway projects to armed forces to national broadcasting, social programs, or the flag, the route for English Canadians has entailed use of that state. To weaken or dismantle it is to strike a blow at our identity.[19]

For Resnick, the dismantling of Canada would have come about precisely as a combined effect of free trade and Meech Lake. He adds that "English Canada has forged an identity based upon strong identification with the institutions of the federal state." In culture, for example, the CBC, NFB, and Canada Council were created in large part to resist American influence.

If English Canada rejected Meech Lake because of its potentially decentralizing nature, it opposed free trade because it reinforced continental integration. In both cases, federal government powers, which were seen as fundamental to Canada's future, were considered to be threatened.

For English Canada, the signing of the Free Trade deal was genuinely traumatic. Growing continental economic integration was quite rightly seen as having major consequences on the country's economic, political, and cultural autonomy.

In economic terms, greater fiscal and monetary harmonization are inevitable over the medium or long term. Broad fluctuations in the value of the Canadian dollar in relation to the American would destabilize the economic environment by offering few long-term guarantees about the viability of investments on either side. Similarly, the Canadian tax system must to a large degree adapt to the American system, otherwise companies located in Canada would be tempted to set up in the United States. Finally, there is a risk that government programs which create imbalances in the free circulation of goods and capital, including purchasing policies, support for regional development, financing for innovation and research and development, marketing boards, and initiatives by state-run industries will be called into question. Generally speaking, it is easy to predict that the state's room to manoeuvre, which to a large degree defines both Canadian and Québécois distinctness, will eventually be narrower and more reduced than it is now.

Politically, the combined effects of fiscal harmonization and the budgetary crisis will lead to heavy pressure to reduce social programs, whose scope and relative "generosity" are seen as key elements in the distinctiveness of Canadian society as compared with the United States. Because Canada's higher tax policy is the keystone for these programs, they will inevitably be threatened in the years to come. Unemployment-insurance reform and a re-examination of the exclusively public nature of medical insurance are signs that the process is already underway.

Because historical justifications for Canada's existence, i.e. the desire of the British empire to "protect" part of British North America against the American Revolution, have long since disappeared, it is easy to understand English Canada's political concerns. Moreover, Canadian policies have tended to conform closely with American policies, particularly in the last decade. Canadian foreign policy, for example, is more often than not a pale copy of Washington's.

In the view of many Canadians, it was state intervention that enabled the country to survive in spite of unfavorable geographical, demographic, and climatic factors. And it is state intervention that still in large measure defines the country's relative autonomy. Similarly, there is a conviction that state withdrawal from economic, social, and cultural life would lead to the disappearance of Canada. That is why free trade was so dreaded and why English Canada was prepared to launch a crusade to save federal government powers.

At the cultural level, there is no lack of challenges either. Although English Canadians turn out high quality cultural products, they still feel they must convince others – and themselves – that these reflect a truly distinct society, one based on specific and enduring values, despite being under siege in North America. The retort – a correct one – is that the Americanization or internationalization of culture is a universal phenomenon that does not affect only Canada. In Europe and Mexico, where the national cultures are relatively strong, it appears possible to absorb the changes related to Americanization while maintaining the components of cultural distinctness. In contrast, for fragile cultures with hazy outlines such as English Canada's, the challenge seems especially tough in the context of constantly expanding economic and political overlapping.

During the 1970s, the federal government made special efforts to fight Americanization and to support Canadian culture. Resnick writes:

In the cultural field, the 1970s were to see the ending of tax exemptions on advertising in the Canadian editions of magazines like *Time* and *Reader's Digest*, and a set of policies to encourage filmmakers, book publishers, and arts groups of various sorts. More significantly, from my point of view, Canadian literature, theatre, dance, and music came of age, not unlike what Quebec had experienced in the 1960s.[20]

Similarly, with respect to the economy, there were attempts to counter the American stranglehold on the manufacturing and natural resources sectors. The question of foreign ownership was the main preoccupation of several government reports (the 1968 Watkins Report, the 1970 Wahn Report, and the 1972 report of a task force led by Herb Gray) and eventually led to federal government adoption of a series of measures, notably the Foreign Investment Review Agency (FIRA) and the Canada Development Corporation (CDC).[21] However, the election of Brian Mulroney and the free trade treaty with the United States would, to a great extent, bring these embryonic national economic policies to an end.

According to Christian Dufour, English-Canadian identity is anti-American in its very essence. "If the Quebecers as a collectivity have remained at the Conquest of 1760, English Canada has never recovered from the defeat of the Loyalists, at the hands of the Americans, only fifteen years later."[22] Whence the fairly widespread sense in English Canada that the Québécois betrayed Canada through their support of free trade in the November 1988 election. This apparently indicated a flagrant indifference to Canadian cultural security in the face of the Americans.[23]

For a large number of English Canadians, then, a strong central government is the main instrument in responding to the challenges of Americanization and building a strong national identity. From this point of view, the division of powers inherent in Canadian federalism and duality may actually present obstacles to pan-Canadian nationalism. On the other hand, it's certainly not up to the Québécois, who have been defending a strong provincial state since Confederation and particularly since the Quiet Revolution – and for essentially the same reasons – to contest the legitimacy of this aspiration. This is true even though, during the referendum campaign, most provincial premiers came and paraded around Quebec to tell us that everything was possible within renewed federalism, including a significant decentralization of federal powers. Mulroney, for his part, and it was what brought about his ruin, has for some years represented a more "provincialist" view of Canada. The leading lights of the country, including most New Democrats and federal Liberals, prefer a strong central state, capable of holding back the American threat, preventing the dismemberment of the country, and guaranteeing Canadians a minimum of autonomy. It is altogether plausible, given the current state of affairs, that Quebec would be more hindrance than help in a Canada in search of its own distinct society. Bela Egyed, a Carleton University philosophy professor, maintains; "The advantages to English Canada of political separation are evident ... The 'break up' of English Canada is a more serious danger than separation from Quebec. This process of breaking up has been taking place already because the federal government has been paralyzed by Quebec in its effort to deal in a meaningful way with problems unique to English Canada."[24]

Part of the opposition to Meech came from the observation, often confused and contradictory but no less real, that English Canada can no longer simply rely on Quebec to ensure its own distinct character. For some English-Canadian nationalists, including the writer Margaret Atwood, Canada can exist without Quebec. It should not be surprising that Jean Chrétien's statement during the Liberal leadership campaign to the effect that English Canada would not survive and would probably join the United States should Quebec separate aroused such indignation among our compatriots in the English-speaking provinces.

A CANADA OF REGIONS: MYTH OR ALTERNATIVE?

After the failure of Meech Lake, a number of Canadians and Québécois proposed reconstructing Canada on the basis of strong regional governments associated in a decentralized confederation.[25] This notion obviously runs counter to that of a strong central government. It seems, however, to agree with some of the preoccupations put forward by the Reform Party and of BC Premier Bill Vander Zalm, who favours a form of sovereignty-association for his province.

No matter what political status Quebec chooses for itself in years to come, there is no doubt that regionalism will continue to exist in Canada, and that the Maritimes and the West, for example, could find it advantageous to unite into regional governments. It is far less obvious, however, that the new regional authorities would "replace" a strong federal government or favour reduction of the central government's powers.

When the Maritime provinces joined Confederation, they were the most prosperous, most dynamic colonies in British North America. Geographic and economic factors, as well as a federal national policy that favoured central Canada, led to the region's decline. At the present time, the Maritime provinces are the poorest region of the country and are experiencing a situation of chronic under-development and under-industrialization. The unemployment rate is the highest in the country, investments are weak, and there is strong migration to the rest of Canada.

This situation obviously creates a sense of alienation and frustration toward the federal government, which is held responsible for the current dead end. Moreover, reliance on federal equalization payments has reached a point where the Maritimes really have no choice other than to make a statement of faith in federalism and a strong central government. Any weakening of Canada's spending power or its economic room to manoeuvre would necessarily mean a reduction in transfer payments, including unemployment insurance, family allowance, old-age pension benefits, regional development grants, and funds associated with cost-sharing and equalization agreements. In the case of Newfoundland, for example, equalization payments inflate provincial government revenue by 65 percent. It's not surprising, then, that Clyde Wells should have been so insistent about the need to maintain a strong central government.

It is in the West, on the other hand, that regionalism has developed most in recent years, and where it forms the most credible threat to a centralized federal government. As is the case in the Maritimes, the sense of regional alienation is based on a perception that the Ottawa government is first and foremost the instrument of central Canada, more particularly Quebec. Indeed, more often than not French Quebec serves as a scapegoat for western rancor: "If regional rivalries are normal in a federal regimem it is still revealing to note that, in the Prairies, Quebec remains the favourite target, while Ontario continues to profit more practically from federalism."[26]

Unlike the Maritimes, however, the western provinces have a relatively strong economic basis for their regional or autonomist demands. Well provided with raw materials and energy resources, they are turned toward the American market, profit increasingly from the new economic vitality of the Pacific, and would undoubtedly be better served economically by more direct ties with the United States. Historically, they have relied on the support of interventionist provincial governments (particularly the CCF and NDP) and have participated in numerous federal-provincial squabbles over control of natural resources, notably potassium (Saskatchewan) and oil (Alberta). The federal government's National Energy Policy, which fixed the price of Alberta oil below the international price to encourage the industrial base of central Canada, especially Ontario, was seen as a veritable hold-up.

Even in the West, however, there are limits to regionalism. On the one hand, the region is far less monolithic than we think. Manitoba, for example, a poor province lacking major natural resources and strongly dependent on federal transfer payments, continues to demand a strong central government able to equalize opportunities and revenues between the provinces. Gary Filmon was very clear on that point during the Meech Lake debate. On the other hand, as far as language, culture, and values in general are concerned, the population of the West is fully assimilated to the anglo-Canadian entity. Polls show clearly, moreover, that a very strong majority of the citizens of these provinces is opposed to any annexation to the United States, despite whatever economic interest this might represent. Finally, in political terms, western regionalism is unquestionably mainly a sign of the region's alienation from central Canada and its absence of power at the federal level. The western provinces could live with a strong and effective central government, to the degree that it provided a better representation of their interests and an improved balance of power. Accordingly:

Contrary to Quebec, the West has never seriously considered leaving the country. Its ultimate goal is not even the increase of the powers of the provincial governments. Far from wanting to be an outsider, this region aspires to a more complete integration into the system. It asks that federal policies seriously take into account its concerns ... What the West wants [is] to influence the central power in the sense of its own priorities, which are essentially economic.[27]

It is likely, moreover, that the sovereignty of Quebec would bring Ontario and the western provinces together on a more egalitarian basis.

ENGLISH CANADA IN THE FACE OF QUEBEC SOVEREIGNTY

I do not share the opinion that "the collapse of English Canada will be an inevitable conclusion of the independence of Quebec."[28] In my view, the process of redefining the structures of the Canadian state which was started "in a roundabout way" during the debates on Meech, will lead to long and arduous discussions. But even if we are still far from a consensus, the desire to survive, to resist Americanization, and to rely on a relatively powerful federal government to do so can only lead to a new Canada in the years to come.

Once again, Quebec will be the key mechanism in this process. English Canada is becoming increasingly aware of the fundamental incompatibility between its vision of the country and Quebec's. This attitude is expressed in part by a greater "openness" towards sovereignty. According to a Gallup poll conducted early in June 1990, three out of ten Canadians (29 percent) supported this option for Quebec.[29] These figures are clearly higher than those recorded by Gallup before the 1980 referendum.

Rejecting the political consequences of Quebec's distinctness and the concept of two nations as an integral part of Canadian federalism does not mean, however, that English Canada refuses any new *modus vivendi* with Quebec. More and more English Canadians now realize that a fundamental redefinition of relations between Quebec and the rest of the country would be in their interest. The day after the failure of Meech, Resnick wrote that, "the sovereignty of Quebec within a confederal union with Canada would make it possible to reconcile the desire of a vast majority of English Canadians for a reasonably strong central government, and that of the Québécois for the strongest government possible."[30]

Former Newfoundland premier Brian Peckford declared that "Quebec should now become politically more autonomous, while remaining economically associated with the rest of Canada."[31] Daniel Drache and Mel Watkins wrote in *The Globe and Mail* in favour of a binational solution with separate states.[32]

Ultimately, the dénouement of the interminable Meech Lake saga will signal, for English Canada as much as for Quebec, a new start towards a fundamental – and very necessary – redefinition of the political frameworks of Canada and Quebec.

Sovereignty and the Future of French

Obsessed with the problem of defining themselves as a society distinct from the United States, that intrusive, spoilsport neighbour, many Canadians have nonetheless been adamant that the Québécois did not constitute a distinct society.

Along with other Québécois, during the finest hours of the Meech sideshow I took part in endless discussions in English Canada about the underlying meaning of that concept. With a hint of annoyance and a touch of aggressiveness, my English-Canadian friends never missed an opportunity to remind me that the Québécois go to McDonalds as much as they do, that they're terribly materialistic, that their lifestyle and values are typically North American. Of course we pointed to our authentically Québécois cultural production, distinct from that of Europe or America. It's well known that the Québécois, unlike the French from France, can write and sing rock music in French. We managed to find some subtle differences in our behaviour too: an approach to economic development that involves more cooperation and state control, for example. When we wanted to upset them a little, we'd mention our liberal attitudes and our greater tolerance (confirmed by numerous polls) towards homosexuality, abortion, and, of course, the anglophone minority.

All of that can be defended and there are those who do it very well. It must be admitted that beyond the self-image we might prefer we are still to a large degree North Americans, so that more than any infinite variations in behaviour and values, the French language remains one of the dominant character-istics of the Québécois identity. Consequently, of all the reasons evoked to support Quebec's sovereignty, maintaining and developing our language head the list.

In looking at the development of attitudes in Quebec over the past fifteen years, one is struck by an apparent contradic-tion. On the one hand, the image we project is dynamic, inno-vative, and turned towards the future. As attested by their significant support for free trade, Quebec's business people and the society as a whole are rapidly and enthusiastically opening up to the continent and the world. There is, however, another vision of a Quebec that is anxious and nervous about its future, whose linguistic and cultural insecurity cause it to reject insti-tutional bilingualism and to call for massive legislative protec-tion. These two visions don't divide the Québécois into two opposed camps, but they still co-exist in most individuals, faith-fully reflecting the realities of modern Quebec. Although they aren't always easy to reconcile, they flow logically from one another. The extensive opening onto the continent and the world is inevitably accompanied by vigorous demands for pol-icies to support the language and culture.

In the context of a sovereignty to be built, it seems more important than ever to review the sources of Quebec franco-phones' linguistic insecurity, of the historical and legislative contexts that prevailed during the evolution of our language legislation, and the place of francophone minorities in Canada, as well as that of our own anglophone minority.

IS FRENCH IN QUEBEC STILL THREATENED?

Historically, the survival of francophones in Quebec has been guaranteed by a high birth-rate and the relative isolation of its population. Today the demographic situation and Quebec's geo-political and cultural integration into North America are the main sources of insecurity.

The birth rate has fallen from 4.3 children between 1956 and 1961 – one of the highest in industrialized countries – to 1.5 between 1981 and 1986, which is not even enough to replace the population. In 1987, the lowest birth rate in our history was recorded, 1.35 children. An increase to 1.60 was noted in 1989. It is still too soon, however, to assert that this is a significant reversal of trends. It is clear, in any case, that current rates still do not permit the maintainance of the francophone population. In addition, many immigrants still choose English as the language of use.

If birth rates and migratory movements are unchanged, the population of Quebec will start to decline at the beginning of the next century, or in less than ten years. Demographers estimate that in fifty years, the number of francophones will be no more than 4.8 million. To this we must add that Quebec's share of the population of Canada, which was 29 percent in 1951 and only 26.5 percent in 1981, will shrink even further, dropping to about 24 percent in 2006. A decline in Quebec's political influence within Canada will inevitably follow. Moreover, according to Michel Paille, a demographer with the Conseil de la langue française, the proportion of francophones in Quebec as a whole, which was 83 percent in 1986, has stopped increasing and will decline by 1996. In Montreal, for example, francophones could form 57 percent of the population in 1996, as compared with 60 percent in 1986 and 64 percent in 1951. In theory, there could be attempts to reduce the number of new immigrants. In practice, however, Quebec – even more than the other provinces – desperately needs to increase its demographic weight and slow down the aging of its population.

Another phenomenon which is important for the future of French in Quebec, is that North America will not escape the growing trend towards the creation of regional and continental economic groupings. This increased integration will inevitably have consequences for the political and cultural autonomy of

Canada and Quebec, despite the relative protection afforded by a distinct language and culture. When J.R. Ewing of "Dallas" speaks French, and Céline Dion and other Québécois performers aspire to the American big time by singing in English, and Jean-Pierre Coallier mimics NBC's David Letterman, there are smiles of course, but these are also concrete signs of the scope of the challenges Quebec must meet if its distinctness is to survive. This is not a matter of passing judgment, even less of condemning: it is simply an observation on how matters stand.

Although institutional bilingualism will no doubt lose ground in Quebec, there is every reason to believe that individual bilingualism among francophones will continue to increase. Whatever political status Quebec chooses in the years to come, this trend will very likely continue to grow. Even more than Europeans, for whom English has become the essential second language, a growing number of Québécois will, if they want to avoid marginalization and be able to play the North American game, be able to get along in English. Many parents in fact are exerting pressure along these lines in our schools.

Quebec francophones are in a state of permanent linguistic and cultural immersion in the anglo-American universe. According to an investigation by the Conseil de la langue française in 1985, 59 percent of records and cassettes purchased by franco-Québécois in the three previous months were in the English language. Of those questioned who were between eighteen and thirty, 64 percent bought more records and cassettes in English than in French. Four out of ten films had been seen in English by francophones, and 30 percent of time spent watching television was devoted to programs in English. Not to mention the fact that increased bilingualism will lead to even greater consumption of American cultural products.

Quebec is not only steeped in North American culture but also in its science and technology. Firms which manufacture computer equipment and scientific instruments are largely non-francophone, and Quebec is very dependent on the United States in this area. High technology equipment is usually presented in English and operates in English. Indeed, through article 144 of Bill 101, the Office de la langue française authorized a large number of head offices and research centres to operate in English.

Over the medium and long term, there is also a risk that the free trade deal with the United States will pose a significant challenge to the French language in Quebec. The economic norms stemming from the agreement may well impose their own priorities, which will run counter to linguistic norms in the many fields where these two aspects are present and possibly in competition. It is conceivable, for example, that norms about the presentation of products covered by the agreement would be safe from a US charge that linguistic constraints on labelling constitute a non-tariff barrier. More important, it seems likely that the broader economic integration resulting from free trade will accentuate the pressures on French as the language of work.

ARE LANGUAGE LAWS EFFECTIVE?

On 27 June 1968 the school board of Saint-Léonard, in the northeast section of Montreal, passed a resolution which made French the language of instruction for all first-grade students. A serious linguistic crisis resulted, including violent confrontations at the beginning of the 1969 school year. In an attempt to settle the problem, the government of Quebec passed Bill 63, which confirmed parents' right to freedom of choice in the language of instruction.

Faced with growing francophone dissatisfaction, the government decided to create a commission to investigate "the situation of the French language and linguistic rights in Quebec." The Gendron Commission, which tabled its report in 1972, chose not to deal with the language of instruction, preferring to wait a few years until it had a better idea of the effects of Bill 63. However, having noted that only 64 percent of francophones worked in their language, the commission placed greater importance on this problem.

Meanwhile, immigrants were continuing to send their children to English schools in great numbers. Pressure from public opinion and the 1971 census, which pointed to the sharp demographic decline of francophones across the entire country, encouraged the new Bourassa government to pass Bill 22 in 1974. The bill proclaimed French as the only official language of Quebec and dealt with the language of instruction, of public administration, and business. A French language board was created to encourage employers to adopt a "francisation" program, under pain of not receiving grants or government contracts. Moreover, the law required children who wanted to receive their instruction in English to pass admissibility tests, which aroused considerable discontent among francophones as well as anglophones and allophones, though for different reasons.

Bill 101, or *La Charte de la langue française*, was passed in 1977, only a few months after the election of the Parti Québécois. This bill testified to a clear desire to promote and reinforce the French language – and francophones themselves. To do so, it limited access to English schools to children with at least one parent who had attended an English school in Quebec. The charter also included transitional measures to avoid dividing the children in a family, as well as special dispensations for persons living in Quebec temporarily. As far as the language of work was concerned, the Office de la langue française established a mechanism for the *francisation* of companies. Contrary to the provisions of Bill 22, the practice was no longer optional: all firms with fifty or more employees were obliged to comply with a *francisation* program. Bill 101 clearly indicated the goals of *francisation*, established details and time limits for implementation, and determined sanctions against offenders, which were, all in all, very limited.

The *francisation* program established the necessary steps to insure that employees of a firm could work in French and that internal communications between management and staff, as well as between workers themselves, would be carried out in French. Firms must have a hiring and promotion policy in keeping with the goals of *francisation*. And catalogues, instruction and manufacturing manuals, as well as instructions posted on machines were required to be in French. Finally, firms were required to present themselves in French, using that language in their advertising and in communications with customers, suppliers or the public at large.

The charter was also concerned with giving Quebec a French "face." Accordingly, signs and printed advertising matter would henceforth be only in French. The public service, public utilities, professional corporations and their members must make their services available in French. They could, however, communicate in another language with individuals who applied to them.

In concrete terms, what were the effects of Bill 101 on the linguistic situation in Quebec? Unquestionably, the charter had its most positive impact on the language of instruction for immigrants. In 1976, when the law was about to come into effect, 16.6 percent of all pupils in Quebec were studying in English. Ten years later, there were only 10.4 percent. Moreover, the percentage of allophones attending English schools dropped from 85 percent to 36 percent in 1986–87, marking a clear reversal of trends, considering that Bill 101 was not retroactive and that it allowed children legally enrolled in English schools when the law was passed to continue being educated there, along with their younger siblings. In the Montreal region, 76 percent of school-children born outside Canada were enrolled in French schools in 1982–83, against only

23 percent when the law came into effect. Finally, a government study published in June 1990 showed that 81 percent of allophones attending French schools were still studying in French at the CEGEP level. In 1989, allophones constituted 39 percent of the total student population in francophone CEGEPS, compared with 14 percent in 1980. There had been considerable progress, but the fact that English still occupies an important place in communications between students enrolled in multi-ethnic francophone schools remains a sizable challenge.

The French language charter was relatively effective in giving Quebec a French face. Thanks to Bill 101, French has become established in corporate names, on billboards, store signs, advertising posters, and commercials, as well as on road signs. The vast majority of products offered in Quebec now include presentation in French, both on labels and in catalogues and advertising leaflets.

Some progress has also been achieved in *francisation* of firms, particularly as far as internal communications, circulation of French terminology in all sectors of work, and the increased participation of francophones in the higher echelons of business. The proportion of francophone executives and company directors moved from 64.9 percent in 1971 to 69.1 percent in 1981. Income gaps between francophones and anglophones have diminished since 1970. Similarly, since 1961 there has been marked progress in the number of firms owned by francophones. Nevertheless, 50 percent of anglophone executives in Montreal still worked only in English in 1979, compared with only 32 percent of their francophone counterparts working solely in French.

According to the Office de la langue française, almost 40 percent of Quebec firms affected by Bill 101 still do not have a *francisation* certificate. A survey conducted by the Office in 1988 revealed that 54 percent of *francisation* committees were considered to be slightly or not at all active. Fifty-eight percent of firms were devoting only seven and one-half hours per year or less to the committee's activities. It should be noted as well that only firms with fifty or more workers must apply a *francisation* program approved by the Office, and firms not affected by the law represent more than half of the workers in Quebec.

In April 1989, the Office de la langue française published the results of a study by Jolicoeur et Associés entitled "Le français, langue de travail, une nécessaire réorientation." This report showed clearly that *francisation* was still being implemented very slowly both in big business and in the smaller firms, and recommended concerted action by employers, workers, and the state to revive *francisation*. Among its conclusions, it stated that the use of computers and automation as well as documentation in English from suppliers all curb the use of French in business. It was also noted that "the presence of anglophones and the high rate of bilingualism among francophones have created habits of communication very difficult to modify, with English as the norm."[1]

To date, Claude Ryan, minister responsible for the application of Bill 101, has not followed-up on the report, nor has he shown much inclination to make any headway in the dossier. Yet the language of the workplace and the *francisation* of companies will be determining factors for the future of French in Quebec. This is where linguistic balance and the capacity of the francophone majority to create the conditions necessary to support the French language will be played out. In fact the language chosen by allophones will depend essentially on the language of money, the language you have to know to get a good job and build a career. The imbroglio surrounding the language of signs and Bill 178 only serves to conceal the lack of courage and political will on the part of our elected officials in this area that is so crucial for our future.

If the Québécois are afraid of massive immigration and sometimes still practise ethnocentric behaviour, it is because they are aware of their vulnerability where language and culture are concerned and doubt their ability to attract and truly integrate new arrivals into francophone Quebec. Part of the problem stems from the fact that immigration is still a jurisdiction shared between Ottawa and the provinces. Quebec must gain full powers in this area. Obviously, sovereignty would remove the ambiguities and send immigrants a clear message about the French character of Quebec. It is also necessary to improve language training, which has been shown to be essential for the integration of allophones. The Quebec minister of cultural communities and immigration could do far more about attracting immigrants who already speak French or who are capable of becoming francophone.

In fact, Canada and the federal government have never formed a rampart for the French language in North America. On the contrary, ever since Trudeau the federal government has seemed far more concerned about the fate of the anglo-Québécois minority and the francophone minorities outside Quebec. Ottawa has been deaf to the very real threats to franco-Québécois cultural integrity and security. The federal government has, moreover, devoted considerable energy and resources to contesting and reducing the impact of Bill 101.

Actually, in the years following passage of Bill 101, several judgments have considerably weakened its impact. In March 1984, in the Miriam case, the Court of Appeal ruled that an employer is obliged to use French only when communicating with all of his staff, not his employees individually. In the Sutton case of August 1983, the Superior Court ruled that a patient wishing to obtain a medical report in French from a professional must make his request before the report is written.

Even more important, in December 1979 the Supreme Court declared chapter 3 of the charter, which deals with the language of legislation and justice, to be unconstitutional. This chapter was judged to be contrary to article 133 of the BNA Act which requires that all of Quebec's laws be written and passed in both languages and stipulates that any person has the right to use French or English before the courts. In July 1984, the Supreme Court rendered chapter 8 of Bill 101, on the language of instruction, inoperative, holding it to be incompatible with Article 33 of the 1982 Constitution Act. In fact this judgment substituted the "Canada clause" for the "Quebec clause" in Bill 101: that is, it would henceforth allow access to English schools to children of parents who had received their primary education in English anywhere in Canada. Moreover, the judges of the highest court in the land recognized that Article 33 had been formulated precisely to counter the provisions of Bill 101 on the language of instruction. Finally, in a judgment rendered on 15 December 1988, the Supreme Court established that articles 58 and 69 of Bill 101, insofar as they prohibit the use of languages other than French in commercial signage, advertising, or corporate names restrict "commercial" freedom of expression.

WHEN DEMOGRAPHERS TURN POLITICAL ...

Because the future of the French language has become one of the major political justifications for Quebec's sovereignty, debate on the matter has become considerably politicized in recent years. English Canadians and some francophone federalists have used every trick in the book to deny the very existence of the demo-linguistic threat hanging over the francophones. Certain demographers and statisticians occasionally choose to drop their scientific claims and blithely indulge in barnyard propaganda, thereby placing themselves in a highly ambiguous position.

After some inelegant side-steps that put him in opposition to the majority of demographers, Réjean Lachapelle, chief statistician at Statistics Canada, concluded in a speech delivered at Queen's University in December 1989 that "in every respect, the situation of French has improved both in Quebec and in certain other provinces."[2] He based this extraordinary conclusion on the following factors: a rise in the inter-generational transmission of French as a mother tongue, an increase in the proportion of French-speakers among non-francophones, and the growing attraction of French schools.

As Lachapelle himself admits, his analysis does not take into account some key elements in the demo-linguistic situation of francophones, namely a low birth rate and the negative impact of immigration. On the rise in inter-generational transmission of French as a mother tongue, Lachapelle notes a clear decrease in the rate of anglicization both in Quebec and in Canada as a whole. Aside from the fact that anglicization is continuing nonetheless, some severe criticisms have raised doubts as to the correctness of this analysis. According to University of Ottawa mathematician Charles Castonguay, the criterion used by Lachapelle – the increased transmission of French from mothers to children – is inadequate. Data based on the relationship between mother tongue and the language actually spoken at home that make it possible to observe directly the evolution of linguistic assimilation at home among members of the same family are much more pertinent, and they show no significant slowing down in the rate of anglicization of young adults in Canada with French as a mother tongue between 1971 and 1986.[3] Improvement in the intergenerational transmission of French does not seem to be accompanied by a corresponding drop in the rate of anglicization of francophones who have reached adulthood, for either men or women. Before drawing any final conclusion about the rate of anglicization in Canada, this paradox will have to be explained.[4] Is it necessary to point out the number of Canadians of French-speaking ancestry who also use English at home?

In addition, the movement that Lachapelle notes can be explained by progress in assimilation itself, and not necessarily because the position of French has improved. Indeed:

as francophones outside Quebec are assimilated to the English language and the residual francophone population is increasingly concentrated in Quebec, the proportion of francophones "submitted to the risk" of anglicization, according to standard demographic vocabulary, is reduced. It is the rate of anglicization for Canada overall that must slow down then, failing the arrival of large numbers of new easily assimilable francophones outside Quebec.[5]

It is essential, therefore, to measure the extent to which the gradual decrease in the assimilation indicator for all of Canada can be explained by the fact that francophones are more inclined to remain in Quebec than in the past, before we conclude that the position of French has improved. As Castonguay points out, similar considerations apply to the anglicization of all the "francophone minorities outside Quebec. As New Brunswick francophones, who are clearly more resistant to assimilation, represent, in the wake of the faster assimilation of other francophone minorities who are more exposed to risk, a growing proportion of francophones living outside Quebec, we must expect a reduction in the rate of anglicization outside Quebec."[6]

With respect to the progress of bilingualism among non-francophones, it is not true that an increase in the number of occasional speakers of French (anglophones) compensates in quality or quantity for the relative decrease of its usual speakers (francophones). According to Castonguay, "the development reported by Réjean Lachapelle represents more the dilution than the diffusion of French in Canada."[7] As for data on the language usually spoken at home, which alone can attest to the current use of French, these figures continue inexorably to drop ... All signs indicate, moreover, that knowledge of French by non-francophones remains largely superficial and in at least one-third of cases does not imply the ability to sustain "a fairly long conversation on a variety of subjects."

The war of numbers and of demo-linguistic interpretations is just beginning. To be continued.

THE FUTURE OF LINGUISTIC MINORITIES

There have been a number of proposals for a territorial solution to settle the linguistic crisis in Quebec and Canada. The classic example, obviously, is Switzerland, where linguistic boundaries separate the German, Italian and French regions in such a way that unilingualism is *de rigueur* in the operation of local government services, schools, and public life in general. Swiss citizens are free to cross linguistic boundaries, but if they do they must expect to change languages, as would an immigrant coming to a new country. The political strategy behind these strict rules consists of separating the languages at the regional level as much as possible and restricting bilingualism or multilingualism to the central government, a strategy that attempts to anticipate contact in order to ward off conflict. Belgium has adopted a similar system, making Flanders a Flemish-speaking region and Wallonie a French region, but it has been unable to apply the Swiss model completely because the capital, Brussels, although in Flemish territory, is predominantly French. Making an exception to the rule of territorial unilingualism, the Belgian capital has been designated a bilingual region.[8]

It is highly possible that one day or another, with or without sovereignty, the force of circumstances will place Quebec in a similar situation. In the name of open-mindedness, pluralism, and tolerance, I personally would prefer a solution that favours the survival of minorities, inside as well as outside Quebec. One of the fundamental requirements of the present situation is an unambiguous stand on the political rights of the various components of Quebec society. Frustrations already built up or those to come, including the inevitable opposition to sovereignty by a large majority of non-francophone Québécois as well as the real danger of an anti-francophone backlash in the English provinces, are liable to get out of hand and create intolerance in Quebec itself. Whence the need for any political project or declaration of sovereignty to clearly confirm the historic place of anglophones, natives, and members of the different

97

ethnic groups as full-fledged citizens of a resolutely French Quebec.

On the other hand, integrating anglophones into Quebec society is liable to be difficult. There is still much to be done here – on both sides. Efforts by anglophones to learn French didn't really start until after the first Parti Québécois victory in 1976. Today, according to a Sorécom poll carried out for Alliance Quebec in May 1990, almost 60 percent of anglophones questioned declared themselves to be pessimistic or very pessimistic about their future in Quebec, while more than one-third believe it is probable or very probable that they will leave the province in the next two years, more than half for political reasons.[9] Fifty-seven percent believe that relations between the two communities are rather poor. This poll also shows that the bilingualization of anglophones does not necessarily guarantee their integration, since over 40 percent of young people with more than 16 years of education – who are therefore the most "bilingual" – believe that they will leave Quebec within two years.[10]

Disturbingly, the poll confirms the sort of apartheid in which francophones and anglophones live. Even in 1990, anglophones still had few or no social contacts with their francophone compatriots; 90 percent said they spoke French with friends occasionally, rarely, or never. It is not surprising, then, that when asked to judge the state of relations between the two communities in the past two years, only 10 percent believed that they have improved. The fact that 51 percent of anglophones use French at work occasionally, rarely or never[11] says a lot about the situation of French as a language of work. It's amazing, then, that when it came time to draw conclusions from this poll, Alliance Quebec placed the burden of the anglophone community's future solely on the shoulders of the majority: "The challenge for Quebec society is to respond to the preoccupations of the English-speaking community and to avoid a new exodus of English-speakers."[12]

It would have been reasonable, it seems to me, to expect the anglophone community to be ready at least to *share* with francophones the challenge of integrating them into Québécois society.

In order to better understand anglo-Québécois behaviour, it is important to remember that since Bill 22 they have been undergoing a profound existential crisis. As francophones have been resolving their problem, that of the anglophones seems to be getting worse. Rather than feeling called upon to respond to the challenge of recent events, they feel that they are being attacked, assaulted, shaken up. They refuse to accept minority status because it was imposed on them by legislative means. The real problem, then, is that the minority status of the anglo-Québécois – to the degree that it exists – remains essentially involuntary.[13]

The current situation of anglophones in Quebec is, to say the least, ambiguous. As part of a majority in Canada and North America, they have trouble accepting minority status. For most anglophones, integration means more than just learning French: above all it means participating fully in and contributing to the society in which one lives. In a speech to an anglo-Montreal audience on 25 April 1990, former Alliance Quebec president Peter Blaikie stated certain truths which, offered by a franco-phone, would probably have been seen as xenophobic. Recalling that in a multi-ethnic society bilingualism is always "the obli-gation of the minority," he deplored that in Montreal today it is still possible to live entirely in English. He maintained that anglophones must henceforth identify with Quebec first if they expect to have a place in the Quebec of tomorrow: "Until we think of ourselves as Quebecers, it's going to be very difficult for us."[14] To do this, Blaikie asked anglophones to integrate them-selves into the Québécois political dynamic as well, by joining one of the existing parties – including the Parti Québécois.

In fact, though, only a sovereign Quebec offers the possibility of a true reconciliation between the two communities.[15] Once the burden of institutional bilingualism has been lifted and ambiguities about the language chosen by ethnic groups are gone, francophones will find some security. On the day the

English language is no longer seen as a threat to francophones, it will undoubtedly enjoy more room to manoeuvre in a Quebec that is more tolerant of its minorities. For francophones themselves, English will be seen more as an instrument of power on an anglophone continent. We can even dream of the day when we will be able to get along without crutches like Bill 101. As René Lévesque put it so well, languages laws are essentially "humiliating" for those who pass them.

It has been said repeatedly that anglophone rights and institutions are the envy of all the francophone minorities in the country. Anglophones possess and administer a complete, state-financed educational network, including three universities. English is recognized by all courts. The anglophone community controls its own hospital network, while Bill 142 guarantees health and social services in the language etc. This is nothing to be complacent about. The anglophone minority must continue to be treated fairly and equitably, as in any normal and civilized society.

Outside Quebec, the situation is quite different. The francophone minorities are currently living through one of the most difficult periods in their history – which is saying a lot. There was a snowball effect after Sault-Ste-Marie, which helped stir up an already latent intolerance. The period after Meech and sovereignty may not improve matters. We have to recognize that the demographic situation of these minorities is disastrous, despite all the efforts by the federal government, and that in a number of the anglophone provinces the process of assimilation seems irreversible.

In Manitoba, the number of francophones dropped from 40,000 in 1971 to 23,000 in 1986. In Saskatchewan during the same period, francophones declined from 16,000 to 6,000. Despite the arrival of numerous francophone Québécois in Alberta during the oil boom, only 17,000 persons there still speak French at home, compared with 23,000 fifteen years ago. In the Maritimes, except in New Brunswick, 72 percent of francophones have been assimilated.

According to Kenneth McRoberts, a York University political scientist and specialist on language policy, federal government measures, including government services in French and the expansion of the French-language services of the CBC, have had little effect on the pressures on francophone minorities to assimilate. In fact, pressures are tremendous, especially in urban centres: the language of work is English, "mixed" marriages are frequent and almost always unfavourable to the language of the francophone partner, and the English media offer the francophone audience a more diversified and appealing product. McRoberts concludes that, despite government efforts, "the dualist experience is even more marginal today than in 1960."[16]

According to a study prepared by the Official Languages Commission, one out of two young francophones outside Quebec does not obtain the French-language schooling guaranteed by Pierre Trudeau's charter. To varying degrees, francophone parents living in the English provinces are exposed to all kinds of local administrative harassment or to provincial government refusal to give their children the academic instruments they need to be educated in French. And yet various studies have shown for years that the absence of French schools is associated with accelerated assimilation of the francophone minorities.[17] Even in provinces where francophones benefit from a "critical mass," the number of francophone students enrolled in French schools is plummeting. Since 1970, the number of students enrolled in French schools has gone from 115,869 to 93,000 in Ontario, and from 60,679 to 47,000 in New Brunswick.

Beyond the figures, however, there is another reality for francophones in English Canada. Francophone networks are being reinforced, institutions are developing, political involvement is increasingly strong, and their visibility is increasing.[18] In New Brunswick, this development is confirmed by the adoption in 1981 of the Law on the Equality of Linguistic Communities, which recognizes the francophone community's right to distinct cultural, pedagogic, and social institutions. Generally, the principal demand of these minorities is no longer institutional bilingualism but rather the creation of a network of distinct institutions. And it can't be denied that interesting progress has been made in this area, both at the federal level and in some of the English provinces. As well as government measures aimed at maintaining and developing major institutions, such as education, broadcasting, and government services, the communities are developing, through their own initiative and with their own resources, a panoply of community social organizations that form part of the backdrop to the francophone space outside Quebec.

For two decades, the federal government has used the francophone minorities as an instrument of blackmail to combat Québécois nationalism. To a large extent, pan-Canadian bilingualism and the reinforcement of minority rights are elegant pretexts for reducing Quebec's latitude in defending its francophone majority and, more important, for challenging its wish to repatriate the powers necessary to be effective. If Trudeau favoured the development of minorities, it was not out of idealism or generosity or because he felt any special sympathy for francophones outside Quebec; it was rather the result of a cynical calculation. Trudeau's attitude seriously skewed the debate and probably contributed to creating in Quebec a reaction of indifference or even hostility towards francophone minorities.

In 1988, the Saskatchewan and Alberta legislatures repealed a series of linguistic rights that their francophone majorities had enjoyed for more than seventy-five years. Robert Bourassa, who tends to think of himself as the champion of the cause of francophones outside Quebec, and his government came out against these francophones obtaining the right to administer their own schools. At most they were to be given a *droit de regard*, the right to examine the administration of these schools. In all likelihood the government of Quebec, which already had enough constitutional constraints in linguistic matters, did not want to contribute to a further reduction

of its powers in this area, and so the francophone minorities had to bear the costs.[19]

Here, too, it's high time to stop being ambiguous. In the years to come, Quebec must give proof of unfailing solidarity with the francophone minorities. Sovereignty or not, the institutional bilingualism that is being attacked on all sides is in no danger of spreading in the next few years. The *minority code* of tomorrow, which Quebec must support and try to negotiate through every possible means, must focus mainly on promoting a network of distinct institutions for francophones outside Quebec. Not only more effective, this solution will probably be less conflict-ridden as well.

With sovereignty, Canadian anglophones will perhaps feel less "threatened" by francophones. There are no guarantees, however, and there should be no illusions either.

– VII –

The Economy: Sovereignty's Achilles' Heel?

The relative progress made by the French language in Quebec over the past dozen years has been due in part to laws, mainly Bill 101, but also to the fact that the Québécois have taken control of an important part of their own economy. Ownership of a company is still the best guarantee that French will be used as the language of work. There are limits to legislative action, and that will be even more obvious in the future than today. Many of the new challenges to the language, including the free circulation of cultural goods, the speed of international communications, development of new technologies, and pressures by the world economy tend to resist linguistic legislation.

Within the limits imposed by free trade, maintaining Quebec's cultural and linguistic distinctness depends in large part on francophones' economic power and on their government's ability to support local economic initiatives. The economic affirmation that began with the Quiet Revolution must be pursued, and we must not forget that, even within a federal framework, for some thirty years now Quebec has been to a large degree the motor of its own development. More often than not, in spite of "French Power," the federal government has contributed remarkably little to the province's economic development. Of course Quebec has received its share of unemployment insurance and old-age pensions, of infrastructures too, but industrial investments and long-term economic spin-offs have too often eluded it.

Everyone has heard the argument that Quebec sovereignty would run counter to world development, especially the trend to bring people together. This is one of the most tenacious myths of recent years. As early as the 1980 referendum, the federalists managed to pass themselves off as disciples of modernity and openness toward the world, with the sovereignists presented as "provincials" condemned to isolation and turning in on themselves.

Economic integration and, to a certain political extent, the political integration of peoples – the European Common Market, for example – doesn't necessarily preclude the flourishing of regional languages and cultures, on the condition of course that they enjoy significant political autonomy. The Catalans in Spain and the Scots in the United Kingdom are ardent supporters of European integration, because they see it as an opportunity to free themselves in part from the oppressive yokes of Madrid and London. Similarly, continental economic integration through free trade is seen in Quebec as a way to reduce economic and political dependence on Canada, which would give Quebec more latitude for enhancing its own distinctness. While we shouldn't under-estimate the challenges that go along with economic integration, it is not inconsistent with the revaluation and reinforcement of national groups. In short, the starting point for Quebec and the European countries may be different, but the result is liable to be the same: cultural sovereignty and political autonomy within a continental common market.

In economic terms, Quebec now has all the assets needed for political sovereignty: a strong, autonomous financial network, a broad industrial base controlled by Québécois, a healthy governmental financial structure, and reduced dependance on the federal government and the Canadian economy.

QUEBEC'S ECONOMIC POWER

Since 1976, I have written a great deal about the spectacular rise of francophone economic power in Quebec.[1] It is clear that this is one of the most important changes of the past twenty years and one of the most lasting consequences of the Quiet Revolution. Even if business people generally are reluctant to transform this new economic power into political power, with the goal of achieving sovereignty, the new economic situation makes a powerful contribution to giving the Québécois the means to choose their political status more freely.

At the dawn of the Quiet Revolution, only 47 percent of Québécois were working for francophone bosses. By 1978, establishments under francophone control were providing 54.9 percent of jobs, while in 1987 this figure increased to more than 60 percent.[2] There is also an important qualitative dimension to francophone progress in business. In the early 1960s, Quebec firms were concentrated almost exclusively in the "soft" sectors, including lumber, leather, and food. Today, there is a strong francophone presence in financial institutions and in the more productive manufacturing sectors, including electrical supplies, transportation material, and aeronautics. In the financial sector, Quebec now controls major pools of capital – assets of $44 billion for the Groupe Desjardins and $38 billion for the Caisse de dépôt – which give francophone firms in the manufacturing sector better access to various sources of financing. In the manufacturing sector, francophone growth is due in part to takeovers: in 1986 and 1987 six Québécois firms – Québecor, Cogeco, Métro-Richelieu, Canam Manac, Télémédia and Hypocrat – made over forty acquisitions and appear among the fifteen most active buyers in Canada.[3] Finally, the main engineering firms – Lavalin, Groupe SNC, Groupe LGL, Roche – and the leaders in computer services – Groupe DMR, Group [G] and IST – are under francophone control.

Business success has led people to forget that it was largely due to the Quebec state that many businesses have been able to take off. Since 1960, massive government interventions have been the driving force behind the development of most

Québécois firms. The role of state-owned industry has been of prime importance. By reorganizing sectors that were losing momentum (pulp and paper, textiles, naval, etc.), by supporting development in those sectors deemed essential for long-term economic development (electricity, gas, steel, etc.), by creating or giving rise to new economic activities (petrochemical, aluminum, etc.), these corporations have played an important role in structuring the economy. On the other hand, state-owned corporations have allowed Québécois firms not only to survive movements towards economic concentration and modernization during the 1960s and 1970s but also to become stronger in relation to Canadian firms in all economic sectors.

Indeed, since 1960 the vast majority of firms located in Quebec have benefitted to varying degrees from help from state-owned corporations. This assistance has taken various forms: salvage operations, financing with or without participation, grants, support for concentration and reorganization, contracts, building of infrastructures, a variety of incentive measures (for example preferential electricity rates), etc. Certain firms owe their very existence to stated-owned corporations, notably Provigo, Pétromont, Marine, Cegelec, Volcano, and Forano. Others, such as Bombardier, SNC, Lavalin, Culinar, Normick Perron, Canam-Manac, Papiers Cascades, Bussière Transport, and La Vérendrye owe a good portion of their consolidation and expansion to public corporations. And stated-owned corporations have been influential in enabling a number of Quebec corporations to escape foreign control.

Recent events clearly show that the state still plays an essential role in the progress of francophone firms and of the Quebec economy in general. During the summer of 1989, for example, the Caisse de dépôt ensured a favourable outcome to the "Steinberg saga," preventing the giant Quebec food chain from falling into the hands of the Ontario conglomerate Oxdon. With the financial support of the Caisse, it was Socanav chairman Michel Gaucher who took over Steinberg. Gaucher made a ten-

year commitment not to sell the firm to non-Québécois interests. Almost simultaneously, the Caisse enabled the Auberge
des Gouverneurs Inc. to buy back the Grand Hôtel de Montréal
from an American insurance company. Finally, in October
1989, the Caisse invested $112 million in convertible deben-
tures to allow Pierre Péladeau to buy Maxwell Graphics of the
United States for a price of $500 million, thereby becoming
the second largest printing interest in North America. For the
Caisse de dépôt, this was "an opportunity to invest in the international development of a Québécois firm."[4] Maxwell Graphics
holds the printing contracts for *Time* magazine and for airline
flight schedules. Neither Gaucher, Péladeau, nor the owners of
the Auberge des Gouverneurs would have had sufficient financial resources to complete the transactions in question on their
own.

In recent years, however, business people have become more
independent-minded and many have not hesitated to question
the state intervention that in large measure brought them into
the world. However, Quebec's industrial structure is still
largely deficient, the technological revolution is far from being
complete, and the gap between Quebec and Ontario is still
very considerable. The gains are fragile and the private sector
has proven incapable of presiding single-handedly over the bal-
anced economic development of the province or of taking up
the challenges now facing Québécois society.

Even where Quebec control is concerned, the battle has not
been won and in all probability never will be. The proliferation
of mergers and acquisitions in 1989, notably the sale of Con-
solidated Bathurst to Stone Container of Chicago and of the
Groupe Commerce to Nationale Nederlanden of the Nether-
lands, should give pause. Québécois firms are still relatively
small and thus liable to takeovers. With free trade, especially
if there is a marked economic slowdown in the coming years,
caution and vigilance are essential. American or other foreign

takeovers of a number of local firms would be disastrous for Quebec. The maintenance and development of capital reserves to permit intervention to safeguard control of certain firms, and the development of Québécois-controlled firms in specific sectors, notably those related to culture and the transmission of values (communications, radio, newspapers, TV, advertising), natural resources, financial institutions, public transportation, aeronautics, micro-electronics and other advanced technologies must be, more than ever, on the agenda. Given the current state of affairs, this strategy cannot be put to work without active state support.

The discussion over the past few years on the virtues of free enterprise and privatization must, at the very least, be put into context. If Quebec wants to survive culturally and linguistically and contend with regional rivalries and an increasingly unstable and difficult international situation, while continuing to compensate for market forces when these develop in a direction contrary to its economic and political interests, it must not only preserve but also continue to refine its main instruments for economic intervention, which include stated-owned corporations.

FROM CANADIAN MARKET TO FREE TRADE[5]

Within the continental economy, and despite the progress made since the Quiet Revolution, Quebec is still in a situation of double dependency. Quebec's economic development, like that of the rest of Canada, has occurred in large part along the lines of American economic interests, giving rise to important shortcomings: a weak manufacturing structure, a strong dependence on the export of raw materials, overdevelopment of the tertiary sector, and underdevelopment of scientific research. Within Canada, on the other hand, Ontario's political power and the control it exercises over the federal state have enabled that province to make its own economic development a priority, to the detriment not only of Quebec but also of the West and the Maritimes.

Whatever the historical responsibilities of Quebec's traditional elites for this double dependency, Ontario has been able to orient the country's internal economic development and to "manage" Canada's dependency on the United States to its relative advantage. As an intermediary or a privileged mediator between the American and Canadian economies, Ontario has been able to obtain the bulk of the "beneficial" spin-off from continental economic integration. Indeed, this is one factor that explains Quebec's under-development.

It is important to recognize that Ontario's economic domination is not due to coincidence or to purely geographical or technological factors. The federal government's economic policies have greatly helped Ontario to take advantage of its geography and other "natural advantages." Note among other things the steel policy, the Borden line, the auto pact, transportation policies (railroad and seaway), and policies for establishing American subsidiaries. In short, by attempting to build an "unnatural" country and artificially reorient continental economic relations along an east-west axis, Ontario has managed to harness the other provinces to its advantage.

The economic consequences of Canadian integration for Quebec include control of a good part of the internal Quebec market by Ontario interests and an overdependence on light industry, with Ontario keeping the lion's share of heavy industry for itself. Moreover, Canadian firms established in Quebec have behaved just like some American companies in Canada, with the same negative effects for the Quebec economy. These firms have siphoned off profits and savings accumulated in Quebec and concentrated their research and development and head-office activities at home (more often than not in Toronto). These tendencies have increased as Quebec has become more aggressive in its demands for a bigger piece of the economic pie.

The way in which Quebec's economy is integrated into the American economy is qualitatively different from its integration into the Canadian economy, and this is due not solely to the size or relative importance of Quebec's two "partners" but also to the form this dependency takes. Dependence on Canada is more immediate and, in a certain sense, more easily reversible. Canadian companies control mainly those sectors of the domestic market that produce goods for common consumption, as well as "intermediary" sectors whose development is closely dependent on and related to American capital. These sectors include commerce, food and agriculture, financial and other services, transportation, iron and steel, communications, and textiles. For its part, American capital is concentrated in sectors that are generally heavily internationalized, integrated, or based on "advanced" technology.

Attempts to develop and reinforce Quebec capital have come up against markets that are already saturated and an economic space that is largely dominated by Canadian and American companies. It soon became obvious that Canadian capital was the most immediate obstacle or, more positively, that there were possibilities for expanding francophone economic power in sectors dominated by Canadian companies. It is not surprising that during the 1960s and 1970s Canadian companies bore the brunt of Quebec's policy of acquiring control over its domestic market. At the same time, Quebec was trying to reinforce its economic ties with the United States in exports and capital as well as technology. As early as 1977, two studies prepared by the Office de planification et de développement du Québec concluded that "a closer connection with the United States seems to be the most realistic and most natural solution for Quebec."[6]

After the referendum defeat, which may have been, in part, the result of excessive dependence on the Canadian economy, the Parti Québécois government sought to intensify economic relations with the United States. It tried, for example, to distance itself from the federal government by endorsing American criticisms of the Foreign Investment Review Agency and the national energy policy. In 1983 Bernard Landry, who was then Quebec's minister of external trade and international affairs, declared that free trade accorded well with the sovereignist objectives, and came out in favour of a US-Canada-Quebec common market. During a visit to the United States two years later, René Lévesque foresaw that the liberalization of trade between Canada and the United States would be the most important issue in the coming years.

Following the Tokyo Round of the General Agreements on Tariff and Trade (GATT), which reinforced the process of world economic integration, Canada-US free trade became, in a sense, inevitable. The free trade deal will undoubtedly speed Quebec's economic "de-Canadianization" and weaken economic ties between the provinces. By reinforcing North-South relations, it will reduce Quebec's economic dependence on Ontario even further, thereby making the sovereignty of Quebec much more plausible. Already, today, 35 percent of Quebec's exports go to the United States, compared with 25 percent to Ontario.

In addition, Quebec's support for free trade stems from the conviction that federal policies of economic nationalism favour Ontario's manufacturing industry to the detriment of Quebec's industrial structure, which is still largely centred on resources. These policies make Quebec an "annex" of the Ontario industrial core. It is not surprising then that Ontario, which risks losing part of its captive pan-Canadian market to the United States, should have opposed free trade. Ontario's interests lie more in the direction of an unhampered national market than in continental free trade. Even the Toronto-Dominion Bank did not hesitate to admit, in a confidential report prepared in 1990, that "Quebec's economy has prospered in recent years thanks to the spirit of entrepreneurship and direction of the francophone managerial class" and that "Quebec will in all probability derive more advantages from the Canada-US free trade treaty than will any other province."[7]

In 1980, the Quebec government and Quebec entrepreneurs already possessed, to a large extent, the tools necessary to bring about sovereignty. Developments of the past ten years have made economic association with Canada less essential for Quebec, and it is very likely that relations between Quebec and the Canadian provinces will eventually be similar to those between Quebec and the United States. Nevertheless, economic relations between Quebec and Ontario are still very important and whatever the eventual political status of Quebec, the mechanisms of economic union will have to be maintained, at least during a transitional period. A sudden split would deal a heavy blow to both economies. The most obvious interdependence exists at the level of markets and exports. But it should not be forgotten that numerous companies controlled from Ontario but located in Quebec would be hard hit by a radical separation.

This explains the haste with which David Peterson and Robert Bourassa let it be known just days after the failure of Meech Lake that it was "business as usual." The two premiers met in Montreal on 26 June 1990, and again in Toronto on 6 July. In Toronto, Bourassa reassured Ontario business leaders that Quebec intended to pursue industrial and commercial exchanges, while Peterson declared that political differences should not harm the $30 billion in trade between the two provinces and the tens of thousands of jobs that are derived from them.

It is significant too that a few days after the failure of Meech, a number of Quebec business people spoke out in favour of a Quebec-Ontario common market. According to Sobeco president Yves Guérard, "Ontario and Quebec could clinch alliances in numerous sectors, such as finance, insurance, transportation, construction, and free trade."[8]

IS FEDERALISM PROFITABLE?

To listen to Gary Filmon, Clyde Wells, and a good many English Canadians, Quebec in recent years has become "the spoiled brat of Confederation." Every time Quebec obtains a favorable economic decision from the federal government – the CF-18 maintenance contract or the space agency, for example – there is usually a great hue and cry in the rest of the country. The idea that Quebec receives preferential treatment is a myth, and one that is damaging to the economy of Quebec.

If Québécois business people are favourably inclined towards the United States and enthusiastic about free trade, it is partly because of the English-Canadian establishment's anti-Québécois and anti-francophone chauvinism. There are numerous examples of the negative effect of such attitudes: Bill S-31, which was aimed at protecting Canadian Pacific from a Quebec takeover; the exclusion of the Caisse de dépôt from the floor of the Toronto Stock Exchange following the takeover of Domtar, the battles surrounding contracts for frigates and CF-18s; the outcry that greeted Power Corporation's attempts to take control of Argus; Air Canada's refusal to sell Nordair to Québecair; the Toronto media's fierce resistance to federal grants to stimulate the General Motors plant at Sainte-Thérèse; and the federal government's refusal to permit sale of the Gulf refinery to Gaz Métropolitain. As sociologist Arnaud Sales has pointed out, "When the Québécois bourgeoisie challenges the Canadian establishment, it has a lot more problems than if it sets up in New York."[9]

In addition, according to a major address by Jacques Parizeau at Johns Hopkins University on 27 April 1990:

Fundamentally, a good number of business people in Quebec have changed their perspective. They have understood that with appropriate costs, prices, and exchange rates it was easier and much more profitable to sell in Boston, New York, and Chicago than in Winnipeg,

Vancouver, and Halifax, Toronto being situated more or less between the two. In other words, Canada is no longer seen as a privileged market or, for so many business people, as the only market.[10]

If economic federalism was once profitable for Quebec, that is no longer so today. In 1980, 30 percent of Quebec government revenue came from federal funds; in 1992, it is estimated the figure will be 18 percent. Since 1986, Quebec has paid out more to the federal government (through direct and indirect taxes) than it receives in the form of the purchase of goods and services or transfers to individuals, firms, and the provincial government. In 1988, Ottawa received $1.3 billion more from Quebec than it returned. Because of the very high federal deficit, the federal government imposed a draconian reduction in transfer payments to the provinces and lost any room for manoeuvre on which to base effective socio-economic intervention. These cuts will inevitably affect the federal government's "mission" in equalization payments. In addition, the establishment of a federal GST is an unacceptable encroachment into a field of taxation that has traditionally been the responsibility of the provinces.

In some areas, Quebec loses out inside the present federal regime. In research and development, for example, between 1973 and 1987 Quebec obtained only 17 percent of federal funds while Ontario received 47.6 percent, as well as having almost 90 percent of federal government scientific laboratories on its territory. Since 1987, Quebec's share has remained stagnant at about 10 percent. This phenomenon is all the more disturbing because for some years Ottawa has been spending more than $4 billion per year on scientific activities. In July 1990, federal minister Benoît Bouchard acknowledged that Quebec had not received its fair share of grants, even in strong sectors such as aerospace, pharmaceuticals, or telecommunications.

The monetary policy and high interest rates dictated by the Bank of Canada have also been harmful to the Quebec economy. Thomas Courchene, former chairman of the Ontario Economic

Council, has described the current monetary policy as an Ontario policy that is aimed at preventing the overheating of the economy of southern Ontario, where unemployment is below 5 percent, but which is counter to the interests of the other provinces, where unemployment is higher and economic activity less dynamic. Courchene thinks that the federal government's favourable prejudice towards Ontario is broadly based:

Since Ontario could generally count on the federal government furthering the province's interests, Ontario has been (and still is) in favour of a strong central government ... On the industrial side a strong central government was also desirable because Rideau Street came to be viewed as an extension of Bay Street ... Ontarians looked to Ottawa to legislate in the national interest, which was generally in Ontario's interests.[11]

Quebec's deficit in relation to the national economic accounts must be assessed not only quantitatively but, above all, qualitatively. In fact, the net effect of federal spending in Quebec has been to perpetuate Quebec's under-industrialization as compared with Ontario. The federal government has been content to make transfer payments in order to sustain Quebec's purchasing power. However, probably to avoid harming Canadian companies in Ontario by creating competitors for them in Quebec – particularly in the heavy industry sectors – federal expenditures have contributed very little to the industrial development of the province. Even the Pépin-Robarts Report in 1979 declared that "the evidence confirms in part the current contention that central government expenditures have been concentrated in income support measures, while the province has been receiving a disproportionately small portion of funds to generate employment."[12]

ECONOMY AND SOVEREIGNTY

Most observers who followed the 1980 referendum campaign agree that economic arguments, particularly those aimed at the insecurity and fear experienced by many Québécois, played a decisive role in the final outcome. Will the economy be the Achilles' heel of sovereignty the next time too?

At first glance, the new balance of power and the new economic situation I have briefly described should favour a more serene climate and enable voters to make a decision based on essentially political motives. The final months of the Meech Lake debate should have convinced even the most reluctant that a sovereign Quebec would be economically viable. Almost unanimously opposed to sovereignty-association in 1980, many business people have spoken out along these lines. As emphasized by Pierre Laurien, vice-chairman of the board of Merrill Lynch, "Quebec has the economic security necessary to make a choice according to its convictions. Quebec made a choice in 1980, at a time when it was still uncertain about its economic future. Today, that uncertainty has been dispelled."[13]

Even more surprising, during the debate on Meech numerous financial institutions, American as well as English-Canadian, notably the Bank of Montreal, the Toronto-Dominion Bank, and Merrill Lynch (US), published highly reassuring analyses of the economic impact of sovereignty. For Merrill Lynch, the biggest brokerage firm in the US, the independence of Quebec should not have major long-term effects on the big international money markets and "the diversification of the Quebec economy ... will compensate for the jolts that a certain form of sovereignty could provoke in the short run."[14] According to a Bank of Montreal report, Quebec has all the legal, administrative, and economic tools it needs to face eventual independence, and "Quebec's economic momentum should continue no matter what its political future."[15] Finally, the American division of the Toronto-Dominion Bank states in a confidential report that Quebec will still be a favourable place for investors regardless of the outcome of Meech Lake.[16]

But let's not be naive. Today, as in the past, economic blackmail is still the best weapon of the opponents to Quebec's sovereignty. A good part of the population of Quebec is still fearful.

A *Globe and Mail*-CBC poll carried out in late June 1990 showed that 62 percent of Québécois supported sovereignty, but that 41 percent expected their standard of living to deteriorate should Quebec become independent.[17] A major economic offensive should therefore be expected. Other reports and other declarations, perhaps even from the same financial institutions, will probably point out the risks and instability inherent in any change of political status.

The arguments are predictable. If Quebec suggests monetary union, as is likely, English Canada will let it be known that it does not want this. If there is an attempt to create our own currency, the bugbears of devaluation and instability will be brought out. It will be maintained that the sovereignty of Quebec would shut Canada out of the G-7, the economic forum of the seven most industrialized nations. No reference will be made to the fact that Canada's influence in the G-7 is, if not non-existent, then at best marginal. It will be suggested that the United States won't allow the Free Trade Agreement to apply to a sovereign Quebec. And yet, as Jean-François Lisée has pointed out, "if tomorrow Ottawa attempted to shut an independent Quebec out of the Canada-US free-trade agreement, American interests would oppose this fragmentation of the large continental market."[18]

During the Meech Lake debate business people, in league with the federal government, launched an extraordinary campaign of economic blackmail in an attempt to shake up the recalcitrant provinces and break English Canada's strong opposition to the accord. Hundreds of newspaper articles and television reports predicted a drop in the dollar, declining investments, and rising interest rates should Meech fail. None of that happened. In the weeks after the fateful deadline, the Canadian dollar actually reached unequalled heights, the Montreal and Toronto stock markets rose, interest rates began to fall by late July 1990, and both Moody's and Standard and Poor's, the American brokerage firms, announced that they intended to maintain their ratings for Quebec government bonds.

Thus the bleak predictions by business and the federal government were not fulfilled. In the post-Meech period, they were the first to claim, contrary to what they had been saying for months, that the accord's failure would have no impact on Canada's stability and economic prosperity. English Canada was able to a large extent – and to its credit – to resist economic blackmail. Will the Québécois in turn avoid letting themselves be manipulated by the horsemen of the Apocalypse?

– VIII –

Sovereignty: Myths and Prospects

Since the failure of Meech, some Québécois have been mistaking their dreams for reality. They seem to think that the Quebec Liberals, in a sacred alliance with the Parti Québécois, the Bloc Québécois, and the business community, are preparing to lead us towards new political horizons, to autonomy, to the "super-structure," even to sovereignty. But the sovereignty of Quebec is far from inevitable.

Pierre Trudeau was correct on at least one point: it is urgent that the Québécois arrive at a decision. I share his impatience. The debate on Quebec's political and constitutional status has gone on long enough. We must start devoting our best energies to the challenges of this century as quickly as possible: the environment, poverty, health, the building of a lasting peace. The constitutional struggles of the past two decades, which have too often seen us begging for crumbs, have belittled us as a people.

English Canada too wants the Québécois to make up their minds. Through the Meech Lake debate, the options for Quebec have clarified: the status quo or some form of sovereignty. For twenty years we have been lost in a sea of ambiguity. For a long time English Canada and the federal government appeared sympathetic to Quebec's aspirations (the reports of the Royal Commission on Bilingualism and Biculturalism, the Pépin-Robarts Report, etc.) and to an in-depth renewal of federalism. And yet, scarcely eighteen months after the victory of the "No," the new Canadian constitution, adopted in spite of the joint opposition of the Péquiste government and the Quebec Liberal Party, dramatically demystified the promises made by Prime Minister Trudeau and by English Canada as a whole.

With the arrival of Jean Chrétien as leader of the federal Liberals and possibly of the country, there is a risk that the constitutional guerrilla warfare will drag on and continue to threaten the economic stability of all of Canada. If Meech Lake had been ratified, the Canadian breach could probably have been sealed off for another few years. Now that there is no question of Quebec's being satisfied with the status quo, and with English Canada having no intention of accepting any sort of "compromise" in the foreseeable future, sovereignty seems like the best guarantee of stability and the clearest option for getting out of the constitutional morass. This is all the more plausible because now it is English Canada, by developing a vision of the country that is diametrically opposed to ours, who has pushed us aside.

WHAT SOVEREIGNTY?

Should sovereignty be achieved, the redefinition of Quebec's political status could be summed up more or less as cultural and political sovereignty in a North American common market. Cultural sovereignty, i.e., full powers over language, immigration, communications, and education, is not negotiable because it is essential to meet present and future cultural and linguistic challenges, as well as to clearly establish Quebec's identity. The North American common market is self-evident: it is the logical outcome of current economic integration and of the free trade treaty. Economic association with the rest of Canada seems equally inevitable, at least as a transitional measure. In the short term, in fact, both Quebec and English Canada will have to meet investors' concerns, which will be reflected in the value of the dollar and the prices of transferable property and bonds. For the moment then, fear of instability is dictating a thoughtful and cautious attitude.

It is unquestionably at the political level, particularly for institutions and regarding division of powers, that the scenario is hardest to write. That is where the bulk of the negotiations will take place – and where sovereignty will take a "soft" or a "hard" form. Many questions must be asked. Will defence be shared? Will there be a minorities code? Will the free movement of persons, capital, and manpower be absolute? Will there be agreement on one or more political "superstructures" that will lead to creation of a shared federal Parliament composed of elected members and endowed with certain powers? Each side will have to decide whether the goals to be attained should result from privileged relations that go beyond a simple common market, or whether it will be relevant and useful to sacrifice part of its political autonomy.

Until further notice, it is Robert Bourassa who will be in charge of Quebec's political destiny. Therefore we must look to his declarations – which are to say the least ambiguous – about the "superstructure" and the European model for indications about what the immediate future has in store. We must remember, however, that the European Common Market groups together politically independent states that still maintain the greater part of their sovereignty. The Bourassa-style superstructure or the European Parliament flies high, but is very light:

Its budget is minuscule, a little more than fifty billion US for twelve countries, a Parliament whose functions are still symbolic, a decision-making apparatus that resembles our glorified federal-provincial conferences. It will be some time before the member countries [of the EEC] will be anything except States, in the full traditional sense of the term, and political union is still purely theoretical.[1]

Is Bourassa serious when he claims to take his inspiration from the European model? If so, he is contemplating a very wide-ranging sovereignty. Indeed, in such a context the "association" dimension would be very limited. Even the Europe of

1992 does not foresee monetary union, common social or foreign policies, or joint defense. Quite obviously the Europe that Bourassa is thinking about does not yet exist and perhaps never will ...

As for the Parti Québécois, it seems, at the level of discourse at any rate, to want to distance itself from out-and-out sovereignty and to put more emphasis on association. Monetary union and the status quo for military alliances, including NORAD and NATO, are favoured. One week after the failure of Meech, Jacques Parizeau spoke out in support of a Scandinavian-type sovereignty-association.[2] As has already been pointed out, economic association with Ontario seems as inevitable as it is desirable, at least in the medium term. In the longer term, a North American common market seems more probable.

WHO WILL BRING ABOUT SOVEREIGNTY?

In a recently published book, Georges Mathews predicted that Robert Bourassa was going to bring about the independence of Quebec and that after the failure of Meech he would quickly propose a form of sovereignty-association opening into a "new Canadian economic community."[3] The author said he was convinced that the premier of Quebec would be "in a position to make history," and that he would not miss such an opportunity. Mathews also stated that a pan-Canadian referendum would sanction the sovereignty of Quebec and the new economic association. Political scientist Daniel Latouche, for his part, declared categorically that "contrary to what the partisans of Quebec sovereignty may think, their cause will not advance by one centimetre on the day after an English Canadian 'No,' in fact it would be the opposite."[4] Who is correct? I shall try to answer that question, starting with an analysis of the political balance of power over sovereignty in the post-Meech period.

The most positive factor in recent developments is unquestionably the attitude of the Quebec population towards sovereignty and constitutional disputes. Since early 1990,

numerous polls have confirmed that more than 60 percent
support sovereignty. Even after the 9 June 1990 agreement,
when everyone was convinced that the accord was going to be
ratified, a CROP-*La Presse* poll (conducted between 13 and
18 June 1990) showed that 57 percent of Québécois were
still in favour of sovereignty. The "Meech effect," then, moved
about 20 percent of the citizens of Quebec, who described
themselves as "tired federalists," into the sovereignist camp.
As early as March 1989, a poll conducted for the Parti Québécois by Michel Lepage estimated that the 1980 referendum
question would at that moment have had the support of 50
percent of the Québécois. During the last months of the saga,
it became obvious that the population of Quebec had gone
beyond Meech and that the contents of the accord were no
longer very important.

The idea of sovereignty is certainly less exhilarating than it
was ten or twenty years ago. But, *pace* Lysiane Gagnon of *La
Presse*, who sees the current attitude of Québécois as passive,
ambiguous, and resigned,[5] I believe their attitude to be one of
serenity, confidence in the future, and the conviction, acquired
at a price, that Canada has become impossible. A divorce, even
a civilized one, is rarely an occasion for rejoicing. Nor does the
extent of the challenge lend itself to celebration.

MYTH NO. 1

Robert Bourassa and the Liberal Party
Will Lead Quebec to Independence

The reaction of the Quebec premier to the failure of Meech
Lake was made public at a press conference on 23 June. To
emphasize the solemn and dramatic nature of the moment
Bourassa, in one of his finest bits of stage management, chose
the Salon Rouge of the National Assembly to make his declaration. "We are at a critical moment in our history. The

death of Meech calls our political future into question," he declared. Many observers saluted the premier's dignity and firmness.

As is often the case, however, the substance wasn't there. Bourassa announced that he was going to boycott the traditional negotiation processes among the eleven governments. Henceforth, he would hold direct discussions only with Ottawa, attempting to arrive at bilateral accords on specified matters such as immigration, communications, and manpower. In appearance, this decision may seem important. *La Presse* in fact fell headfirst into the trap when it ran a banner headline declaring "The End of the Constitution!"[6] Obviously it was Meech Lake that had given up the ghost; the 1867 constitution and the 1982 amendments still applied to Quebec. As political scientist Léon Dion pointed out, "the protective measures set forth by the premier can be effective only in a very limited fashion and for a short period ... the 1867–1982 constitutional framework remains intact. Moreover, the latitude allowed Quebec depends on the good will of the federal prime minister."[7]

As for Bourassa's refusal to participate in future constitutional conferences, the English provinces certainly weren't going to complain about that, having long asked, following the example of Trudeau and Chrétien, for an end to those endless discussions. Has anyone forgotten that it was mainly Quebec who was the "plaintiff" in the Meech negotiations? And in any case, as Gil Rémillard was quick to note, the government of Quebec didn't object to attending federal-provincial conferences "when the interests of Quebec were at stake."[8] Some days later, there was already talk of participating in federal-provincial conferences if it became impossible to reach bilateral agreements with Ottawa. In short, the response would be flexible, very flexible.

As far as bilateral agreements are concerned, don't hold your breath. Under the best estimates, the booty will be modest. At one stroke ridiculing Quebec's claims, Alberta's Don Getty and

BC's Bill Vander Zalm immediately announced that, under these conditions, they too would negotiate with Ottawa as an equal, and with the intention of going after new powers. Ontario's David Peterson of course opposed such agreements. As for Brian Mulroney, the collapse of his popularity in English Canada will no doubt prevent him from granting Quebec any form of "special status" whatever. According to Jeffrey Simpson of *The Globe and Mail*, he risks losing even the little credibility he still has in English Canada if he agrees to play Bourassa's game.[9] In immigration, where a bilateral agreement was signed in early 1991, Quebec Minister Monique Gagnon-Tremblay defined the limits when she announced that "immigration will *always* be a shared jurisdiction with the federal government," and that, in any case, Quebec didn't want all the powers in this area. A good start.

Bourassa, true to himself, has also set down certain "parameters" that would guide him as he sought a new political status for Quebec: to preserve Quebec's economic security, protect the rights of the anglophone minority, and take account of the francophones outside Quebec, while respecting geographical constraints. It all sounds eminently reasonable. It wouldn't take great semantic shifts, however, to confuse these parameters with the arguments used by the "No" side in the past to persuade Québécois to endorse the Canadian option. In any case, the premier made a point of saying that it was premature to talk about independence.

As for Rémillard, who is less subtle than his leader, in an address to the Conseil du patronat du Québec on 26 June 1990, he talked about a twenty-first century that would be marked by federalism, the need for continuity, and the importance of equipping Quebec with a constitution that would not necessarily come into conflict with the federal regime. But even more significantly, he let drop, "if we do nothing, we're dead."[10] Don't forget that brief remark. It says more about the genuine intentions of the Quebec Liberal Party than any assumption or elucubration about a superstructure.

If Bourassa decided at the general council of the Quebec Liberals on 24 and 25 February 1990 to create a committee to examine the post-Meech period, it wasn't simply because, contrary to what he stated categorically several times during the last election campaign, he has no alternative solution, but because above all he wants to be able to avoid taking a stand and having to embark on concrete actions. His strategy is aimed much more at delaying deadlines and defusing the crisis than it is an expression of any will to act. The premier has been very careful to appoint mainly convinced federalists to his constitutional committee.[11]

The Quebec Liberal party seems poorly placed to make the necessary shift. Despite its apparent unity, it remains deeply divided. On one side are the "nationalists," furious at the rejection of Meech Lake, who in the absence of some progress to reinforce Quebec's autonomy could be tempted by the Parti Québécois. On the other side are the "federalists" for whom the failure of Meech is insufficient reason for a fundamental re-examination of the party's constitutional position, and who could set out to create a resolutely federalist political party should Bourassa ever succumb to the temptation to play ball in the PQ's court. The latter include anglophones still loyal to the party, the vast majority of neo-Québécois, and the Trudeauite "remnants" who were sufficiently numerous to get the Chrétien lists through in a majority of the province's ridings.

Ministers like Sam Elkas, Daniel Johnson, Gérard D. Lévesque, and Liza Frulla-Hébert would never want to seriously weaken the federal link. In contrast, others such as Michel Pagé, Marc-Yvan Côté, Yvon Picotte, and Yves Séguin are prepared to make a move in the direction of sovereignty. At their August 1990 congress, the Young Liberals ratified a proposal calling for the political autonomy of Quebec. As for the Liberal electorate, the two factions are about equally divided. According to a June 1990 CROP-*La Presse* poll, 42 percent of Liberals said they were in favour of sovereignty and 51 percent opposed. This puts some doubt on Georges Mathews' statement to the effect that "any commentator expecting the Liberal Party to be the scene of a fight to the end between federalism and sovereignty is being short-sighted."[12]

The publication of the report of the Liberal Party's Constitutional Committee in February 1991 is yet another attempt by the premier to keep his party together by reconciling the irreconcilable. The "Allaire report," which had the effect of a bombshell on English Canada, promotes a very decentralized Canada and proposes, among other things, a veto power for Quebec, abolition of the Senate, transfer of residual power to the provinces, and the elimination of the federal government's spending power in areas of provincial jurisdiction. For the federalists in the party, including Bourassa himself, the report is nothing more than a basis for negotiation that may eventually lead to considerable compromise. For the nationalists, it is perceived as the minimum demands. While it is likely that the ambiguity will persist for a while to come, it is doubtful that it can endure in the long run.

Bourassa has done everything possible to resolve the constitutional issue. He presented minimal demands in 1986, negotiated downwards in 1987, and ratified an unacceptable compromise in June 1990. Bourassa is no more sovereignist today than during the night of 9–10 June 1990 when, in a moment of euphoria, he delivered an emotional profession of faith in Canadian federalism.

Since the burial of Meech, the Quebec premier has been using every possible means to gain time and avoid the issue, hoping the sovereignist wave will finally abate. He is pursuing – very skilfully – the strategy of the sacred union, and he has been able, at least for the moment, to hang on to some important support. Still, the failure of Meech is well and truly the failure of Bourassa and of his constitutional strategy of the past twenty years; it also provides irrefutable proof that he mis-judged the Canadian political situation and that he was wrong to ask Québécois to vote "No" in 1980.

Using the events at Oka and Kahnawake as an alibi, Bourassa delayed setting up the enlarged parliamentary commission on Quebec's constitutional future. If he should bring about the independence of Quebec, it won't be because he wanted to "make history," but because the population of Quebec will have given him no choice.

As for the Parti Québécois, once its opposition to the accord was established, it adopted a rather clever "strategy of silence" during the Meech Lake debate, which was a good choice under the circumstances. On the other hand, since the failure, Jacques Parizeau and the PQ have in a sense been supporting and legit-imizing the Liberals' actions. In doing this, the Parti Québécois is allowing itself to be dragged into a process it does not control, one that could easily lead it onto the slippery slope of compro-mise. The Parti Québécois is worried about having its option "stolen" by the Liberals. Instead, it should be asking what it would do if the Québécois are called on during a referendum to express their opinion on an "autonomist" but not a sovereignist option. Sooner or later the divorce between the Parti Québécois and the Quebec Liberals will come, but to whose advantage? For the moment, Bourassa holds all the cards and he can count on the complicity of the federal government, who might try, when the time comes and if it's capable of it, to throw him a lifeline.

MYTH NO. 2

Federal Impotence

That the federal government is in a difficult position is obvious. Brian Mulroney gambled his own credibility and that of his government, and he lost. In English Canada, he is held responsible for the constitutional skid and his unpopularity rating has attained historic peaks. If he hopes to make a recovery in the anglophone provinces, he must distance himself from Quebec nationalism.

It would be a mistake, however, to believe that the federal government's current disarray will stop him from intervening in the debate on Quebec's future. Mulroney knows very well that, beyond the great statements of principle, Bourassa is one of Canada's best allies in Quebec. The two first ministers never miss a chance to praise one another in public. Apparent concessions can be foreseen, notably in immigration and communications. In fact, if the room to manoeuvre is slight where substance is concerned, in terms of form everything is still possible. We can also anticipate, in the coming months and years, a federal attempt to create a "national consensus" on matters that do not directly affect federal-provincial disagreements, for example, the environment.

With the creation of Keith Spicer's Citizens Forum on the constitution and the Beaudoin Committee on the amending formula, the federal government was clearly seeking to regain some initiative. One can expect that in the fall of 1991 or the spring of 1992, after the various reports have been completed, the federal government will present a comprehensive set of constitutional proposals to the Canadian people and provinces. It is on this basis that new negotiations with the provinces, including Quebec, could begin anew, not solely on the basis of the Quebec government position. The success of this operation remains a long shot, however.

Even if Chrétien has to some extent self-destructed in Quebec through his contemptuous attitude and his smugness regarding Meech, he shouldn't be underestimated either. In 1993, in the midst of an economic recession, with a Conservative government going to wrack and ruin, some Québécois, looking beyond the constitutional question, could well be tempted to vote for the "lesser evil." And once Chrétien was in power, he could launch a counter-offensive – he who has always been for Quebec's five conditions and for "renewed federalism" ... A nightmare scenario? Perhaps.

Still, the message delivered by the Bloc Québécois victory in the 13 August 1990 by-election in Laurier-Sainte-Marie couldn't be clearer. For the first time in the political history of Quebec and Canada, an openly sovereignist candidate was elected to the federal Parliament. For the first time too the Québécois chose not to vote for "an independent Quebec in a strong Canada." Allegiance to Quebec and to sovereignty is now a priority, even at the federal level.

The "mission" of the Bloc Québécois is to raise new doubts about the legitimacy of the traditional federal parties' claim to speak for Quebec. Have we already forgotten that Trudeau justified unilateral repatriation of the constitution precisely on the grounds that Quebec federal MPs had voted in its favour? Following Trudeau's example, Mulroney recalled, during a visit to his riding in July 1990, that he was a spokesman and representative of the Québécois in the same way as Bourassa and Parizeau.

The by-election in Laurier-Sainte-Marie saw the appearance of a new political species that could be described as "federal-sovereignist," which is symptomatic of the strength of the sovereignist option among the Québécois population. In fact, besides Gilles Duceppe of the Bloc Québécois, both the Conservative and NDP candidates declared themselves to be sovereignists. New Democratic candidate Louise O'Neill said it best: "I won't oppose Quebec's moving towards sovereignty. But I'm running in a federal election, for a federal party. That's a drag, but I can't ignore it."[13]

A drag indeed. Highly ambiguous too. And it's a safe bet that we aren't talking about a vanishing species. Can anyone forget Phil Edmonston's fancy footwork when he declared himself pro-

Meech during his election campaign, but as soon as he arrived in Ottawa was quick to line up behind the anti-Meech position of the new NDP leader?

The Bloc Québécois will also give the sovereignist option a legitimate voice in Ottawa. On the likely assumption that one or more supranational structures are created in Ottawa, the "new kids on the block" could play a role in negotiations between Quebec and the rest of Canada, facilitating the transition towards a new political status. On the other hand, the existence of a "Quebec bloc" also entails its share of political risks. Before they left the party, in an act of faith to Mulroney, the Conservative MPs undertook not to destabilize his government. Sooner or later, the members of the Bloc Québécois will have to cut their ties with the Conservatives, for there is a good chance that in the next federal election the Bloc Québécois would damage the Conservatives, perhaps even helping to elect Liberal candidates in Quebec and Chrétien nationally. Still, the main risk is that of defeat. The Québécois tend not to vote for a party that doesn't have a chance of taking power. They like voting for winners. The temptation to vote for an alternative government, and to try to settle other problems – the deficit, the environment, unemployment, etc. – will always be present.

Bouchard has come a long way since he supported Meech, and since he resigned as a cabinet minister and MP in the Mulroney government. Just how far has he come? What kind of sovereignty does he want? What compromises is he prepared to make? All that remains to be seen. His popularity among the Québécois gives him so much influence that his options will be decisive in the coming months.

As I have already emphasized, the federal offensive against sovereignty will be focused once again on economic questions. Appeals to homeland, Rocky Mountains, the Queen, and the sanctity of so-called national institutions won't work any more. A whole range of economic arguments will have to be brought out. As David Olive said in *The Globe and Mail*, "it's the best hope for unity this fragile country has."[14] There will be hints that Ontario will have to choose between the West and Quebec, and that it will choose the West. It will be said that being sovereignist in today's Quebec is unthinkable, what with job losses, factory closings, an unemployment rate almost twice as high as Ontario's, an economy still too dependent on natural resources, etc. It will be predicted that Quebec can't get along without federal "largesse" and contracts, and the example of Bombardier will inevitably be given. It will be announced that Quebec will lose the head offices of Canadian companies, including Bell Canada, Air Canada, and Canadian Pacific. The Quebec political climate will be blamed for the postponement of major new investments. International financiers will express their scepticism. And that's just the tip of the iceberg!

MYTH NO. 3

Business in the Vanguard of the Sovereignist Struggle

The attitude of business people has been one of the most surprising revelations during the Meech Lake debate. In 1980, after all, they came out strongly in support of the "No" and had considerable influence on the outcome of the vote. Now, in contrast, with the intention of using fear to get Meech through, numerous business people declared that a sovereign Quebec was viable. Let there be no illusions about their intentions. Between the viability and the desirability of sovereignty, there is a margin that some people have cheerfully conjured away – although not the majority of business people. Contrary to a myth they willingly maintain, they are not risk-takers. They fervently hoped for ratification of the accord, mostly to ensure the stability of their environment. For the same reason, there are those who will now refuse any serious reconsideration of the present structures.

For that matter, some months before the deadline for Meech there was already a sense that the wind was turning. On 7 March 1990, wanting to maintain calm, Unigesco president Bertin Nadeau wrote, "the failure of Meech Lake would not signify that Canada had rejected Quebec," that "it wouldn't be so dreadful, should the Meech Accord fail, if Quebec were to stick to its position of the 1980s."[15] That same day, in a thinly veiled warning to the Quebec Liberal Party, Ghislain Dufour, chairman of the Conseil du Patronat, described the irritation of the business world: "If the Quebec Liberals persist with sovereignty, they risk losing the traditional support of business circles ... We need an out-and-out federalist party."[16]

On the day when they, like everyone else, thought the accord was going to be signed, business people heaved an almost unanimous sigh of relief. Claude Castonguay, although it was thought that his federalist convictions had been badly shaken, said he was satisfied and that all that was being done was to correct what had not been done in 1982.[17] Louis Arsenault, chairman of the board of the Chambre de commerce du Québec, added that, "the Québécois would have everything to gain by staying in the Canadian confederation."[18]

After 23 June 1990 a strange silence fell over the Québécois business world ... Three weeks later *The Globe and Mail* observed that the silence of Quebec business people, the same ones who had been in the vanguard of the pro-Meech fight, was a "funny thing." In a tone of contempt mixed with irony the writer explained the phenomenon by suggesting that the unfavorable economic situation and the financial problems of the principal Québécois business spokespersons had quickly wiped out "the euphoric rush of nationalist self-confidence."[19] He then did his best to show that Michel Gauthier and Marcel Dutil, among others, were at that moment having serious problems in their respective businesses.

This silence among business people has much more to do with concerns about the future than with their own economic situation. Moreover, the business community is still deeply divided about sovereignty, even though some would undoubtedly benefit from a stronger Quebec state, one that could support their development even more. Sovereignist employers are a majority in the cooperative movement, in state-owned industries, and in francophone-run small and medium-sized businesses. As for those business people who are tied to large anglo-Canadian and American firms, who are still very powerful despite progress in francophone control and still have a preponderant influence in organizations like the Conseil du patronat, they will probably emerge from the shadows and declare themselves as clearly "federalist" when the time comes to make the big choices.

In the best scenario, sovereignty could enjoy the beneficent neutrality of some business people and the support of others. The real question, in fact, is this: when the federal counteroffensive is in full swing, will enough business people stand up and put forward convincingly the genuine potential of a sovereign Quebec?

MYTH NO. 4

Favorable American Prejudice

In 1977, the American State Department concluded, in a study prepared for Henry Kissinger, that there was no doubt as to the economic viability of an independent Quebec. With surprising perceptiveness, the document saw the promotion of bilingualism in the federal public service and the promise of French schools for francophones outside Quebec "as, at best, a first step and, at worst, as superficial modifications."[20] The authors describe Trudeau as a "centralizing federalist" and wonder how much longer the Canadian prime minister can continue to entice listeners with vague references to new approaches to federal-provincial relations, without ever having to clarify his positions.[21]

The document concludes: "As long as there is no solution to its legitimate demands, Quebec will continue to be unstable, to the detriment of United States interests. Consequently, it is in our interest for this problem to be resolved."[22]

In short, even the United States considers that Quebec and all of Canada must now choose. In April 1990 a *Washington Post* editorial stated that the sovereignty of Quebec would put an end to decades of "corrosive" squabbling between francophone and anglophone Canadians. The paper added that Canada "is constantly hovering on the brink of a bitter break-up," and suggested that if Canadians were going to live in a smaller country, they would feel better for it.[23]

In the conclusion to his masterful study of relations between Washington and Quebec under the Parti Québécois government, Jean-François Lisée declares that the United States would have "allowed" the independence of Quebec in 1980, even if they did not hope for it. Because Canada has always been its best ally, the United States would much prefer a neighbour that was "strong and united." On the other hand, assuming a vote in favour of sovereignty: "the United States' interest would therefore have crystallized in one word – association – and Washington would have pressed Ottawa to negotiate with Quebec. Even the New York bankers' and investors' interests would have been served by successful negotiations between Canada and Quebec."[24]

How would Americans react today to the independence of Quebec? According to Lisée, they would see it as a smaller "nuisance" than ten years ago. This is in part because the end of the cold war makes the question of military alliances less pressing than before, in part because the Americans feel reassured about the political orientations of the Parti Québécois and their capacity to govern. And in part, no doubt, because the Americans are much better informed and more sophisticated in their analysis of the Quebec reality than many think.

Some weeks after the failure of Meech, Hydro-Québec's American customers let it be clearly understood that they would continue to do business with the state-run industry, no matter what the province's political status, and that they would have no reservation about buying electricity from an independent Quebec.[25] In short, the Americans could live with the sovereignty of Quebec, but they are still prejudiced in favour of a strong and united Canada. We can probably expect them to adopt a policy of "neutrality" – unless they give in to the temptation to tell us what they think.

MYTH NO. 5

The Unanimity of "Opinion Leaders"

According to Trudeau and Canadian federalists as a whole, the Québécois "people" is neither separatist nor sovereignist. Rather, it has been manipulated by nationalist elites, particularly those who are called "opinion leaders." The debate on Meech Lake offered a glimpse of a very different dynamic. It was in fact the journalists, intellectuals, and union leaders who were now trailing behind Quebec public opinion.

The major union locals, including the CSN, FTQ, and CEQ, kept a low profile during the Meech saga, waiting for the drama to be played out before taking a clear position in favour of Quebec sovereignty when it became obvious that a strong majority of their members now supported that option. With few exceptions, Québécois intellectuals were virtually absent from the debate. Newspaper editorials generally and steadfastly supported Bourassa. *La Presse* and *Le Devoir*, for example, acted as wet blankets, going so far as to hope for and encourage concessions that even the Quebec government refused to make. They supported the Charest Report, the McKenna initiative, the amendments of 9 June 1990, and more. They had no trouble switching from being convinced federalists to resigned sovereignists, depending on circumstances. Their choice has still to be made.

THE PROCESS OF ACCEDING
TO SOVEREIGNTY: A MINE-FIELD?

On the day after 23 June 1990, the Quebec government was in a very difficult situation. With no credibility in Canada, it could not table new constitutional demands. It cannot be repeated too often that if English Canada wouldn't endorse Meech Lake, it would surely never agree to more. After all, English Canada had seen it all before: Daniel Johnson's "equality or independence," Bourassa's cultural sovereignty in the 1970s, René Lévesque's sovereignty-association, etc. Moreover, despite its strong opposition to the 1982 *coup de force*, we must remember that Quebec quickly fell back into line. It's not surprising then that Quebec's declarations about the post-Meech period weren't taken seriously, but were seen as a bluff. In fact, Quebec's credibility outside the province dropped to its lowest level in a long time, and Bourassa himself commanded no respect in the rest of the country. As well, neither the premier nor his party had a mandate to put forward any new constitutional proposals. Since 1987, the Quebec Liberals' constitutional option had been Meech Lake. With the collapse of the accord, the party no longer had a position.

And so a way had to be found to enable the Québécois to participate in working out a new political status. The Parti Québécois and Jacques Parizeau proposed a three-stage process: convening an Estates-General, adopting a Quebec constitution, and, finally, calling a referendum. The Estates-General, to be overseen by a National Commission whose members would be named by the Quebec Parliament, would have several hundred members from a variety of areas. Aside from the elected members, there would be representatives of the business world, unions, the cooperative movement, professional associations, the universities, community movements, artists, native people, ethnic groups, anglophones, etc. Once there was a clearly defined option, the National Commission would call on a Constituent Assembly, elected by universal suffrage, who would have the mandate to draw up a Quebec constitution in conformity with the resolutions of the Estates-General.

Others, including political scientist Léon Dion and journalist Lise Bissonnette, preferred a commission of enquiry. Professor Dion would have the members of such a commission named after consultation with, and with the consent of, the leader of the opposition, so that it would enjoy great credibility with the public. Their mandate would be to consult broadly on how individuals and groups judged the situation of Quebec in the post-Meech context, and what forms of change they recommended. The commission's report would condense the opinions gathered, as well as information drawn from other sources, within a period of six to eight months. This stage would be followed by a solemn referendum enabling the sovereign people to express its will and provide a clear mandate for future negotiators.[26]

At a joint press conference on 29 June 1990 the premier and the leader of the opposition announced that they had concluded an agreement in principle on establishing an enlarged, "non-partisan" parliamentary commission which became known as the Bélanger-Campeau Commission. Its mandate was to carry out public hearings, to consult the key elements of the society on the broad constitutional orientations of Quebec that could lead to adoption of its own constitution. The commission consisted of thirty-six members, including not only elected members but also representatives of constituted bodies, recognized interest groups, and Quebec's constituent communities.

For Bissonnette, the parliamentary commission would be "nothing more than arbiters between clans, a collection of partisan individuals enjoying a truce, rather than a group beyond any suspicion."[27] Moreover, it would enable the Quebec Liberal Party to keep everyone in sight, for it will report to the National Assembly, which is under majority Liberal control. Above all, however, the dice are loaded against sovereignty. There is no guarantee that an eventual consensus will reflect the vision of the majority of Québécois, more than 60 percent of whom now support sovereignty.

Bouchard, one of the members of the commission, believes that this kind of approach has every chance of making better progress than a commission of inquiry, which is a mechanism "too often used by politicians to cool down a hot potato."[28] He claims, moreover, that while the government is directly associated with the commission through its members and, even more, through the premier, it can't help but get the decision-making process underway quickly. He concludes, "in fact, whatever the premier's intentions, the format he has chosen cannot help but thoroughly shuffle the cards and radically call into question the legitimacy and structure of the federal system".[29]

Quite possible, but the "recommendations" of the Bélanger-Campeau commission will necessarily be the product of compromise, aimed at preventing the federalist wing of the Quebec Liberals from jumping ship. And the next stage, negotiations with the federal government, will probably lead to new compromises. Do we really think the Québécois will recognize themselves in the final product that emerges from this process? Is there not a danger that we'll find ourselves stuck with some sort of "new, improved Meech"?

It is absolutely essential that Quebec does not go to Ottawa without a strong mandate. And the only way to obtain it is through a referendum on sovereignty. A resolution by the National Assembly, or a simple election in which too many contradictory elements and feelings inevitably get tangled up, will never have the force and the legitimacy of a referendum. If the Québécois are serious, if they want to be effective, they must persuade Robert Bourassa to let them speak out, clearly and directly. Any other solution will weaken Quebec irreparably.

The coming months and years should be fascinating ones for Quebec. Nothing is certain, everything is possible.

Notes

CHAPTER ONE

1 *La Presse*, 26 April 1980.
2 Ibid., 10 January 1980.
3 Ibid., 11 January 1980.
4 Ibid., 30 January 1980
5 Ibid., 25 April 1980.
6 Ibid., 20 March 1982.
7 Donald Johnson, ed., *With a Bang, Not a Whimper: Pierre Trudeau Speaks Out* (Toronto: Stoddart 1988).
8 Robert Sheppard, "Both Governments Losing Favour in Quebec," *The Globe and Mail*, 5 May 1982.
9 *La Presse*, 19 June 1982.
10 Ibid., 15 December 1982.
11 Gil Rémillard, "Meech complète le rapatriement de 1982 et répare l'injustice infligée alors au Québec," *La Presse*, 27 March 1990.
12 Ibid.
13 Georges Mathews, *Quiet Resolution: Quebec's Challenge to Canada*, translated by Dominique Clift (Toronto: Summerhill Press 1990), 72.
14 *La Presse*, 22 May 1982.
15 See William Johnson, "Constitution Makes Clear Native Rights Must Be Recognized," *The Gazette*, 14 July 1990.
16 See Jacques Hébert, "Legislating for Freedom," in Thomas S. Axworthy and Pierre Elliott Trudeau, eds., *Towards A Just*

Society: The Trudeau Years, translated by Patricia Claxton, 131–47 (Toronto: Viking 1990).

17 See Josée Legault, "La minorité anglophone au Québec: What does English Quebec want?" Unpublished paper, Montreal, Université du Québec à Montréal, November 1989.

18 See Gordon Robertson, *The Five Myths of Meech Lake* (Ottawa: 1990), 22; and Mathews, *Quiet Revolution*, 75.

CHAPTER TWO

1 These two notions themselves refer to the ideas of territoriality and non-territoriality.

2 Including the Rassemblement démocratique pour l'indépendance, the Société St-Jean-Baptiste, and the Parti indépendantiste.

3 Pierre Marc Johnson in "Johnson veut empêcher la signature de l'Accord," *La Presse*, 2 May 1987.

4 An agreement reached between Quebec and Ottawa in 1978 in which the federal government agreed to give up certain prerogatives in immigration matters. The supremacy of the central government in this area was however in no way affected.

5 Lowell Murray in *La Presse*, 15 June 1987.

6 *La Presse*, 6 June 1987.

7 Quoted in Denis Robert, "La signification de l'Accord du lac Meech au Canada anglais et au Québec francophone: un tour d'horizon du débat publique," in Peter Leslie and Ronald Watts, eds., *Canada: The State of the Federation 1987–1988* (Kingston: Institute of Intergovernmental Relations, Queen's University 1988), 154.

8 Brian Mulroney, "La réponse du premier ministre Mulroney à Clyde Wells," *La Presse*, 8 November 1989.

9 *Commons Debates*, 20 August 1987, 8248.

10 *The Gazette*, 12 July 1989.

11 Robert Bourassa, *Débats de l'Assemblée nationale*, 11 April 1989, 5169.

12 As reported in *Le Journal de Montréal*, 6 June 1987.

13 Cited in Gilbert Brunet, "Bourassa est convaincu d'avoir réalisé des gains énormes," *La Presse*, 2 May 1987.

14 *La Presse*, 9 January 1989.

15 Robert, "La signification de l'Accord du lac Meech," 149.

16 Michel Bastarache, "Dualité et multiculturalisme: deux notions en conflit?", *Égalité* (autumn 1987–winter 1988): 64.

17 Ibid., 65

18 Jacques Parizeau, *The Meech Lake Constitutional Accord*, notes for an address to the annual meeting of the Association of Teachers of History and Social Sciences of Ontario, Toronto, 25 October 1989, 6.

19 The criticism of the "new" version of the Meech Lake Accord draws on an article I published in *La Presse*, 18 June 1990.

20 Jeffrey Simpson, *Globe and Mail*, 8 June 1990.

21 *La Presse*, 11 June 1990.

22 Lise Bissonnette, "Un superbe moment pour bouger," *Le Devoir*, 3 July 1990.

23 Gordon Robertson, *The Five Myths of Meech Lake* (Ottawa: 1990).

CHAPTER THREE

1 Gilles Paquin, "Les libéraux reconnaissent le caractère distinct du Québec," *La Presse*, 30 November 1986.

2 Among others, on regional economic development and on recognition of Quebec's international activities.

3 Cited in Jean-Louis Roy, "Unique, le Québec a besoin de protections spécifiques," *Le Devoir*, 19 June 1985.

4 See Daniel Latouche, "L'art de négocier: la version du Lac Meech," *Le Devoir*, 12 May 1987.

5 Cited in *Le Devoir*, 4 June 1987.

6 *Le Soleil*, 11 June 1987.

7 Michel Vastel, "Souffle l'esprit du lac Meech," *Le Devoir*, 28 September 1987.

8 Cited in Mario Fontaine, "Colère et déception chez les groupes nationalistes," *La Presse*, 4 June 1987.

9 Cited in *La Presse*, 6 June 1987.

10 Daniel Latouche, "Un livre oublié," *Le Devoir*, 20 February 1988.

11 Michel Vastel, "Bourassa paiera cher son appui à Mulroney," *Le Devoir*, 18 December 1987.

12 Maurice Girard, "Pawley reconnaît qu'il existe un ressac anti-Québec dans l'Ouest," *La Presse*, 16 March 1987.

13 In "Say Goodbye to the Dream of One Canada," *The Toronto Star*, 27 May 1987.

14 Ibid.

15 Lowell Murray, "Ne rouvrons pas l'Accord du lac Meech," *La Presse*, 11 September 1987.

16 *The Globe and Mail*, 2 June 1987.

17 *La Presse*, 21 May 1988.

18 "Le Manitoba ratifiera l'Accord du lac Meech," *Le Journal de Québec*, 1 November 1988.

19 "Refuser l'Accord du lac Meech, c'est reporter les négotiations dans dix ans, dit Filmon," *La Presse* 17 December 1988.

20 Clyde Wells, "Pas de statut spécial pour le Québec," *Le Devoir*, 20 January 1990.

21 See Jacques Brassard, *Le prix à payer pour le Québec de l'Accord du lac Meech. Bilan des relations fédérales-provinciales. Décembre 1985–février 1989*, (Québec: 1989), 12–31. In it the author estimates the loss of major contracts for Quebec since the beginning of the Bourassa-Mulroney "love-in" at *more than 8 billion dollars*.

22 *L'Actualité*, 1 May 1990.

23 *The Gazette*, 13 June 1990.

24 Including columnists Lysiane Gagnon and Gretta Chambers.

25 See Gretta Chambers, "By-Election: Lucien Bouchard's Candidate the One to Beat," *The Gazette*, 19 July 1990.

26 See Denis Lessard, "Québec a contribué à l'opinion juridique sur la société distincte," *La Presse*, 14 June 1990.

27 *La Presse*, June 11 1990.
28 *Le Devoir*, 23 June 1990.

CHAPTER FOUR

1 See Denis Robert, "La signification de l'Accord du lac Meech au Canada anglais et au Québec francophone: un tour d'horizon du débat public," in Peter M. Leslie and Ronald L. Watts, eds., *Canada: The State of the Federation 1987–1988*, (Kingston: Institute of Intergovernmental Relations, Queen's University 1988), 131.
2 Lysiane Gagnon, "Une sollicitude suspecte," *La Presse*, 18 August 1987.
3 Robert, "La signification de l'Accord du lac Meech," 133.
4 Ibid., 139.
5 The author is grateful here to Josée Legault of l'Université du Québec à Montréal whose research on the anglophone community of Quebec has in large measure inspired the comments on that subject in this work. See in particular "La minorité-majorité anglo-québécoise: une réflexion théorique," *Égalité*, (Autumn 1990).
6 Ibid., 135.
7 "Anglophones Urged to Reassure Canada," *The Globe and Mail* 22 January 1990.
8 Robert, "La signification de l'Accord du lac Meech," 136–7.
9 Yvon Fontaine, "La Politique linguistique au Canada: l'impasse?" in Ronald L. Watts and Douglas M. Brown, *Canada: The State of the Federation 1989* (Kingston: Institute of Intergovernmental Relations, Queen's University 1989), 146.
10 Donald Johnston, ed., *With a Bang, Not a Whimper: Pierre Trudeau Speaks Out* (Toronto: Stoddart 1988), and Thomas Axworthy and Pierre Trudeau, eds., *Towards A Just Society: The Trudeau Years* (Toronto: Penguin 1990).
11 Michel Vastel, *The Outsider: The Life of Pierre Elliott Trudeau*, translated by Hubert Bauch (Toronto: Macmillan 1990).

12 *The Globe and Mail*, "Trudeau Decries Separation Hoax," 27 October 1989, and Patricia Poirier, "Trudeau Plays Down Fears over Quebec Separation," *The Globe and Mail*, 21 March 1990.

13 Paul Roy, "Halifax: Chrétien se sent honoré par les attaques de ses principaux adversaires," *La Presse*, 21 April 1990.

14 Ralph Surette, "Meech, Chrétien et les Maritimes," *La Presse*, 17 May 1990.

15 Lysiane Gagnon, "Où est passé Jean Chrétien?" *La Presse*, 19 June 1990.

16 Jeffrey Simpson, "The Illusions of Those Canadians Who Still Think Quebec Is Bluffing," *The Globe and Mail*, 28 June 1990.

17 *The Winnipeg Free Press*, "Don't Seize the Spirit," editorial, 29 December 1988.

18 Gordon Robertson, *The Five Myths of Meech Lake* (Ottawa: 1990), 13.

19 Hugh Windsor, "Wells Was Lightning Rod for Anti-French Feeling, Polls Show," *The Globe and Mail*, 10 July 1990.

20 Ibid.

CHAPTER FIVE

1 "Le fossé s'élargit entre le Québec et le Canada," *La Presse*, 8 April 1990.

2 *La Presse*, 8 March 1990.

3 *The Globe and Mail*, 12 February 1990.

4 Cited in Hugh Windsor, "Wells was lightening Rod for Anti-French Feeling, Polls Show," *The Globe and Mail*, 10 July 1990.

5 Ibid.

6 Chantal Hébert, "Ottawa retarde de nouveau sa réglementation sur les langues," *Le Devoir*, 7 April 1990.

7 "Sault-Ste-Marie célèbre le multiculturalisme," *La Presse*, 6 February 1990.

8 Neil Morrison, cited by Francine Pelletier, "Bilinguisme: il faut remettre les choses à leur place, à la manière de Laurendeau," *La Presse*, 25 November 1989.

9 Daniel Latouche, *Le Bazar* (Montreal: Boréal Express 1989), 116.

10 Intended in the Anglo-Saxon sense of the word, that is, a reference to a political rather than an ethnic entity.

11 Clyde Wells, "The Meech Lake Accord," an address to the Canadian Club of Montreal, 9 January 1990, 5.

12 Robert, "La signification de l'Accord du lac Meech au Canada anglais et au Québec francophone: un tour d'horizon au débat public," in Peter M. Leslie and Ronald L. Watts, eds., *Canada: The State of the Federation 1987-1988* (Kingston: Institute of Intergovernmental Relations, Queen's University 1988) 153.

13 Wells, "The Meech Lake Accord," 12.

14 Ibid., p. 5

15 Carl Mollins, "An uncertain nation," *Maclean's* (1 January 1990): 13.

16 Sylvia Bashevkin, "Solitudes in Collision," *Comparative Political Studies* (winter 1990). The author cites three polls conducted in 1977, 1979, and 1981.

17 Robert, "La signification de l'Accord du lac Meech," 154.

18 Wells, "The Meech Lake Accord," 5.

19 Philip Resnick and Daniel Latouche, *Letters to a Québécois Friend* (Montreal and Kingston: McGill-Queen's University Press 1990), 29.

20 Ibid., 56.

21 Ibid., 56.

22 Christian Dufour, *A Canadian Challenge/Le Défi québécois*, translated by Heather Parker (Lantzville, BC: Oolichan Books 1990), 150.

23 Resnick and Latouche, *Letters to a Québécois Friend*, 57.

24 Bela Egyed, "Quebec should separate so that the rest of Canada can unite" Unpublished manuscript, Department of Philosophy, Carleton University, June 1990, 12.

25 This was the case notably of *La Presse* editorialist Alain Dubuc.

26 Dufour, *A Canadian Challenge*, 147.

27 Ibid., 135.

28 Kimon Valaskakis, "Le Canada est menacé de divorce et le lac Meech n'est est que la pointe de l'iceberg," *La Presse*, 15 November 1989.

29 "Les Canadiens profondément divisés sur la question de la séparation du Québec," *La Presse*, 3 July 1990.

30 Philip Resnick, "Vers une nouvelle union Canada-Québec," *Le Devoir*, 23 June 1990.

31 Gilles Gauthier, "Peckford souhaite que le Québec devienne plus autonome politiquement," *La Presse*, 24 June 1990.

32 Daniel Drache and Mel Watkins, "A Wholly Undemocratic Process," *The Globe and Mail*, 6 June 1990.

CHAPTER SIX

1 Johanne Lenneville, "La promotion du français au travail: pas facile," *La Presse*, 12 April 1989.

2 Réjean Lachapelle, "Démographie et langues officielles au Canada," 10. Paper delivered at conference "Vers la coexistence équitable et la réconciliation: droits et politiques linguistiques," Queen's University, 8 December 1989.

3 Charles Castonguay, "Commentaire présenté au Colloque international sur la diffusion des langues," 2. Unpublished paper delivered at the Centre international de recherche sur le bilinguisme, Quebec, Université Laval, 9–12 April 1989.

4 Ibid., 3.

5 Ibid.

6 Ibid., 2.

7 Ibid., 1.

8 Jean Laponce, "Pour réduire les tensions nées des contacts interlinguistiques: solutions personnelles ou territoriales?" Paper delivered at Queen's University, Kingston, Ontario, 9 December 1989.

9 Results of Sorécom poll published by Alliance Quebec, Montreal, June 1990.

10 This trend confirms one already observed by Uli Locher in the 1970s in *Les anglophones de Montréal: émigration et évolution des attitudes 1978–1983* (Quebec: Gouvernement du Québec 1988).

11 Sorécom poll, June 1990.

12 Ibid., 7–8.

13 See Josée Legault, "La minorité-majorité anglo-québécoise: une réflexion théorique," *Égalité* (Autumn 1990).

14 Peter M. Blaikie, "The future of the anglophone ethnic minority in Quebec." Speech to Emmanu-el Beth Sholom Synagogue, 25 April 1990.

15 Legault, "La minorité-majorité anglo-québécoise."

16 Kenneth McRoberts, "Going about It the Wrong Way," *The Globe and Mail*, 19 March 1990.

17 Marc Doré, "Un francophone hors Québec sur deux ne peut aller à l'école française," *La Presse*, 27 February 1989.

18 See Yvon Fontaine, "La politique linguistique au Canada: l'impasse," in Ronald L. Watts and Douglas M. Brown, *Canada: The State of the Federation 1989*, (Kingston: Institute of Intergovernmental Relations, Queen's University 1989), 145.

19 Marcel Adam, "Le Québec contre les Franco-Albertains," *La Presse*, 13 June 1989.

CHAPTER SEVEN

1 See, among others, "Les nouveaux paramètres de la bourgeoisie québécoise," in Pierre Fournier, ed., *Le Capitalisme au*

Québec (Montreal: Éditions coopératives Albert St-Martin 1978), and Pierre Fournier, with Yves Bélanger, *L'Entreprise québécoise* (Montreal: Éditions Hurtubise HMH 1987).

2 Philippe Dubuisson, "Les francophones font d'autres gains dans les affaires," *La Presse*, 3 November 1989.

3 Ibid.

4 Laurent Cloutier, "Québecor deviendra le numéro deux de l'imprimerie en Amérique du Nord," *La Presse*, 31 October 1989.

5 This section is taken in part from my article "La souveraineté-association: une stratégie de transition vers l'option nord-américaine," *Le Devoir*, 30 March 1979.

6 Office de la planification et de développement du Québec, *Analyse structurelle à moyen terme de l'économie du Québec* (Québec: Éditeur officiel 1977), 61. See also A. Dayan, *L'Environnement international et le rôle du Québec dans la division du travail* (Québec: OPDQ 1977), 79.

7 Maurice Girard, "La Banque Toronto-Dominion ne craint pas l'après-Meech," *La Presse*, 14 March 1990.

8 Laurent Cloutier, "Les gens d'affaires favorisent une union Québec-Ontario dans un marché commun," *La Presse*, 27 June 1990.

9 Michel Tremblay, "Le nouvel entrepreneurship québécois," *La Presse*, 6 May 1986.

10 Jacques Parizeau, "Le discours de Jacques Parizeau à l'Université Johns Hopkins," *La Presse*, 10 May 1990.

11 Thomas Courchene, "What Does Ontario Want?", 23. John Robarts Lecture, Kingston, Ontario, 1988.

12 *Pépin-Robarts Report*, (Ottawa: Minister of Supply and Services 1979), 75.

13 Laurent Cloutier, "Les gens d'affaires favorisent une union Québec-Ontario dans un marché commun," *La Presse*, 27 June 1990.

14 Maurice Girard, "L'indépendance n'effraie plus les financiers US," *La Presse*, 9 March 1990.

15 Presse canadienne, "La séparation du Québec n'aurait rien d'inquiétant, selon une étude de la Banque de Montréal," *La Presse*, 13 March 1990.

17 *The Globe and Mail*, 9 July 1990.

18 Jean-François Lisée, *In the Eye of the Eagle*, translated by Arthur Holden et al. (Toronto: Harper-Collins 1990).

CHAPTER EIGHT

1 Lise Bissonnette, "Le disciple de Monnet," *Le Devoir*, 5 July 1990.

2 "Parizeau favorise une souveraineté-association de type scandinave," *Le Devoir*, 30 June 1990.

3 George Mathews, *Quiet Resolution: Quebec's Challenge to Canada*, translated by Dominique Clift (Toronto: Summerhill Press 1990), 178.

4 Daniel Latouche, *Le Bazar* (Montreal: Boreal Express 1989), 215.

5 Lysiane Gagnon, *La Presse*, 14 April 1990.

6 "Finie la constitution!", Denis Lessard, *La Presse*, 24 June 1990.

7 Léon Dion, "La longue marche du Québec," *La Presse*, 27 June 1990.

8 Denis Lessard, "Québec a contribué à l'opinion juridique sur la société distincte," *La Presse*, 14 June 1990.

9 Jeffrey Simpson, "A Dilemma for Mr. Mulroney as Mr. Bourassa Devises New Rules," *The Globe and Mail*, 27 June 1990.

10 Paul Roy, "Si on ne fait rien, on est morts," *La Presse*, 27 June 1990.

11 As pointed out by Gilles Lesage in "L'après-Meech du PLQ," *Le Devoir*, 10 April 1990, "Is it a coincidence? We have the sense that the most nationalistic elements in the caucus, those who forced M. Robert Bourassa to resort to the notwithstanding clause for Bill 178 in December 1988, have the smaller

share. We'll see in the months to come if this tool will be of any use, or if it will be used to muzzle those MNAs who want to get off the beaten path."

12 Mathews, *Quiet Resolution*, 14.

13 "Audrey McLaughlin appuie sa candidate 'séparatiste' dans Laurier-Ste-Marie," *La Presse*, 8 July 1990.

14 David Olive, "Times Are Getting Tough," *The Globe and Mail*, 16 July 1990.

15 Cited in *Le Devoir*, 7 March 1990.

16 Cited in *La Presse*, 7 March 1990.

17 Richard Dupont, "Comme prévu, les gens d'affaires sont satisfaits," *La Presse*, 12 June 1990.

18 Ibid.

19 Olive, "Times Are Getting Tough."

20 Jean-François Lisée, "La solution de Washington," *L'Actualité* (15 April 1990): 30.

21 Ibid.

22 Ibid.

23 "La presse américaine supporte déjà les effets de l'indépendance du Québec," *La Presse*, 17 April 1990.

24 Jean-François Lisée, *In the Eye of the Eagle*, translated by Arthur Holden et al. (Toronto: Harper-Collins 1990), 273.

25 Maurice Girard, "Le statut politique du Québec laisse froids les clients américains d'Hydro-Québec," *La Presse*, 12 July 1990.

26 Dion, "La longue marche du Québec".

27 Lise Bissonnette, "Papoter ou réfléchir?" *Le Devoir*, 7 July 1990.

28 Lucien Bouchard, "C'est le bon véhicule, qu'il démarre au plus vite," *Le Devoir*, 10 July 1990.

29 Ibid.